GOD &
CAESAR

CARDINAL GEORGE PELL

GOD &
CAESAR

SELECTED ESSAYS ON RELIGION,
POLITICS, & SOCIETY

EDITED BY M. A. CASEY

CONNOR COURT PUBLISHING PTY LTD
BACCHUS MARSH, VICTORIA, AUSTRALIA

THE CATHOLIC UNIVERSITY
OF AMERICA PRESS • WASHINGTON, D.C.

Published in Australia and New Zealand by Connor Court
Publishing Pty Ltd, P.O. Box 967, Bacchus Marsh 3340, Victoria,
Australia, *www.connorcourt.com.au*

ISBN 10: 0-9802936-8-5

ISBN 13: 978-0-9802936-8-5

Published in the rest of the world by The Catholic University
of America Press, 620 Michigan Ave., N.E., Washington, D.C.
20064, *cuapress.cua.edu*

The paper used in this publication meets the minimum
requirements of American National Standards for Information
Science—Permanence of Paper for Printed Library Materials,
ANSI Z39.48-1984.

∞

Library of Congress Cataloging-in-Publication Data
Pell, George, 1941–
    God and Caesar : selected essays on religion, politics, and
society / George Pell; edited by M.A. Casey.
        p. cm.
    Includes bibliographical references and index.
    ISBN 978-0-8132-1503-7 (pbk. : alk. paper)   1. Christianity
and politics—Catholic Church.   I. Casey, Michael, 1965–
II. Title.
    BX1793.P45 2007
    261.7088′282—dc22
                                        2007005152

For Michael and Ruth

My god-daughter Rachel

Joseph, Simeon, and Miriam

CONTENTS

FOREWORD

Although it was not totally unexpected, Alaric's capture of Rome on 24 August 410, resonated not only in the city itself but throughout the empire. We know that three days of looting, destruction, and massacre followed, though the churches of the apostles Peter and Paul were spared. Thousands of Romans, Christians, and pagans found refuge within its walls though it was also accompanied by a vast exodus which emptied the city. We also know that Jerome lamented the disappearance during those powerfully compelling days of his friends Pammachius and Marcella, two among the anonymous dead. Caught up by the catastrophe Jerome could cry: 'Where is salvation if Rome perishes?' (*Ep.* 123,16).

Rome's capture and fall also resonated in the thought of Augustine, the influential and brilliant bishop of Hippo. His immediate task was to answer the questions and meet the anxieties of the faithful whose own faith had been shaken, especially of those refugees from Rome who had arrived in North Africa. He delivered a sermon on the whole question at Carthage on 29 June 411, but his enduring response, not only specifically to Rome's fall but also to the complex and intricate reality of the significance and purpose of the Christian life lived within an earthly city was to be found in his *City of God*, a text that would remain a critical benchmark upon which generations of thinkers considered many of the issues addressed by Augustine.

The life of the individual Christian and the institutional Church within the state, whatever form that may assume, remains, as for Augustine, an important reality. It is conveniently termed the relationship between Church and State, a relationship that has taken on many forms as the contours of history have unfolded through the centuries. It remains an important issue in contemporary society and now involves not only the Christian Church but also other non-Christian faiths which hold that certain fundamental truths need to be safeguarded and protected within the body politic.

This collection of addresses delivered over several years, on different continents—Australia, Europe, and the United States of America—and to various audiences, reflects many of those perennial questions that characterize the complex and often highly charged relationship between God and Caesar. Cardinal George Pell, archbishop of Sydney, offers an extraordinary insight to and judicious thinking on some of the critical questions that necessarily involve the Catholic faithful as their life is lived out in the political reality of the western world.

Two overriding themes permeate these essays: the specific relationship between Catholicism and democracy and the relationship between fundamental Christian truths and various value judgments promoted and legalized in many contemporary democracies. Of course, the two areas are intimately and inescapably interrelated especially as modern secular democracies arrogate to themselves the right to pass laws that are unambiguously contrary to the truths of Catholic faith and the natural law.

These laws revolve in a particular though not unique fashion on the basic questions of life: abortion, euthanasia, stem cell research, etc. Many of the essays in this book deal with these life issues in a lucid and thought-provoking fashion, illustrating not only the obvious point that such laws are contrary to Church teaching, but rather how they are equally contrary to the good of society itself. One of the central themes, adopted from Pope John Paul II but brilliantly developed by Cardinal Pell, turns on the "culture of death" that these political policies encourage and support. This is not simply a matter of religious enthusiasm or doctrine, though of course it is that, but rather a clarion call to seriously reassess and redirect policies that destroy the very fabric of what it means to be genuinely human and genuinely fulfilled. The role of the Catholic and Christian in this process is complex, especially given the theoretical assumptions so prevalent in much of modern Western democracy and given particular emphasis and cogency by a media that all too often pits itself against any intervention by the Church. Nevertheless, the Church and individuals called to Her, are equally called upon to enter into serious debate and dialogue with contemporary political society, not to impose some form of theocracy but rather to inform society that its "culture of death" inescapably leads to a culture of annihilation, especially for those who are the weakest and least protected.

One of the critical questions remains as to what is meant by the democratic process and the extent to which fundamental Christian principles can or must be included as a basis for specific laws. The contemporary and widespread view holds that the Church cannot impose its ideas on a free contemporary society, but the present collection offers some important correctives to the contemporary and fashionable view: a massive confusion on what is meant by individual conscience; a tendency to privatize belief and consequently to privatize Catholic teaching as if it did not reflect fundamental truths; the importance of clearly stating one's beliefs and in the process encouraging a robust discussion on the real nature of participatory democracy. The simple fact is that the Church has a fundamental role to play in the formation of a country's values, especially through its role in democratic debate. Any attempt to silence the Church's genuine role is perilous for contemporary society.

The world in which these talks were given is dramatically different from that in which St. Augustine wrote his *City of God*. Many of the practical questions are similarly different, but the underlying principles that both determine and nourish the faith of an individual within the Church and which in turn remain critical for the living out of that faith in society, remain the same. St. Jerome would have been calmed if he knew that, despite the moral catastrophe of much of modern western democracy, a churchman had vigorously and intelligently confronted it. He would find such a churchman in Cardinal Pell.

—*Msgr. Brian E. Ferme*

GOD &
CAESAR

INTRODUCTION

Democracy in Australia has been good to the Catholic community, who spread over the entire continent, nowhere constituting even a local regional majority.

Since 1986 Catholics have replaced Anglicans as the largest denomination, a little over one-quarter of the population. They welcomed the separation of church and state, initially as some protection against an Anglican–Protestant majority, quietly ignoring the encyclical of St. Pius X *Vehementer nos* of February 1906, which condemned the separation of church and state as "a supreme injustice" done to God. They realized, as in the United States, that their democracy was fundamentally directed against neither God nor their religion.

Anti-religious passion has rarely burned brightly in Australia. No Catholic church, for example, has ever been destroyed by an Australian mob. Religious practice is lower than in most parts of the United States, but militant secularism is also milder. It has been suggested that the Australian temptation is to trivialize Christ and not to crucify him. Certainly the separation of church and state does not prevent substantial commonwealth and state government money being spent on the capital and recurrent costs of religiously based schools, Catholic, Protestant, Jewish, Muslim, and others.

In most parts of the English-speaking world outside Britain and Ireland, the Catholic faith was planted by Irish immigrants who had no emotional attachment whatsoever to the Crown and the system that treated them so poorly over the centuries in Ireland. There was therefore little sentimental attachment to any alliance of throne and altar as there was in many parts of Catholic continental Europe, and most Catholics over the course of the twentieth century voted with the workers' party, the Labor party, or the Democratic party. This is now changing or changed.

The sectarianism that plagued history in Australia recurrently until after the Second World War was a clash of English versus Irish and Protestant versus Catholic much more than any struggle between secularism and religion, although the most significant tension today is between a secularizing liberalism and a new Judeo-Christian coalition, whose most active members are Catholics and evangelical Protestants.

Australia has no equivalent of Puritan New England in the seventeenth century, not even in the colony of South Australia, and no contemporary equivalent of the Bible Belt in the Southern states of the U.S.A.

Born during the Second World War, which concluded victoriously for the Allies before I was aware of the strife, I was a teenager in the fifties during the height of the Cold War, an admirer of Pope Pius XII and the Catholic cardinals, such as Wyziński, Mindszenty, Stepinac, Beran, and Slipyj, who publicly opposed the Communists.

In my state of Victoria in southeastern Australia, Catholic life was dominated by the archbishop of Melbourne from 1917 to 1963, the Irishman Daniel Mannix. He was an admirer of Pope Leo XIII, believing Catholics had been slow to exploit the opportunities opened to them by democracies and critical of "sacristy priests" who thought that religion should not venture much further than the church building. Like Cardinal Moran of Sydney and Archbishop Duhig of Brisbane, he established himself as a major public figure and used this as one means of encouraging and strengthening Catholic involvement in public life in Australia.

Mannix's central priorities were religious, and at his death in 1963 his flock had a depth of faith and level of religious practice rarely equaled in Christian history. Vocations to the priesthood and religious life abounded. His encouragement of education, which had continued for ninety years without government money through the staffing of the schools by religious orders, provoked a social mobility into the middle classes comparable to—and possibly surpassing—that achieved in the United States.

When he arrived in Australia there were still job advertisements explaining that Catholics and Jews need not apply. The discriminations and separations were real, if generally mild, and he inspired confidence and loyalty in his largely Irish-Australian congregation with his regular commentary on public affairs.

The two greatest controversies of his long episcopate were his successful opposition to conscription in the two referenda of the First World War and his public support of the anti-Communist union activists (who, working from "Industrial Groups" within the Labor party, became known as "Groupers") expelled from the Australian Labor Party after the 1954–55 Split, who then formed the Democratic Labor Party. In the second struggle he was supported by an outstanding writer and political organizer from Melbourne, B. A. Santamaria.

I admired these two men when I was a teenager and I admire them today, fifty years later. They helped inspire me to resist any attempt to privatize Christian and Catholic teaching and provided me with significant intellectual foundations for my thinking. The example and writings of Pope John Paul II also sustained and encouraged me, and countless others, to persist in the struggle, in the culture wars, in the battle against "the culture of death." Initially I did not like this term, thinking it excessive, even provocative, but as we contemplate the spread of abortion (perhaps one-third of Australian women are victims), the enthusiasm for euthanasia, drug-taking and its consequences, and demographic decline everywhere in the Western world, we have to concede that the term is prophetic and accurate.

My central concerns are religious. These philosophical writings are not a substitute for Christ's call to conversion, to repent and believe, but an important corollary, a contribution to dialogue with the surrounding society. History and sociology demonstrate that the great religions produce significantly different societies and cultures. Bad religion of any sort can be poisonous, but my interests are primarily in the Christian and Catholic contribution to Western life.

A few basic convictions run through these essays. Most basic of all is a commitment to and a reverence for reason, a belief that in many cases we can recognize the truth of matters. Without this, discussion across differences becomes platitudinous and even dangerous in the long run.

In his controversial milestone address at the University of Regensburg in 2006, Pope Benedict XVI elegantly stressed the importance of reason in the Catholic intellectual tradition. We are called to an encounter of faith and reason, an encounter between genuine enlightenment and religion, because God himself is reasonable. Reason is the common bridge we travel with those of other religions and no religion as we work to maintain and improve our communities and societies, through both dialogue and debate.

The first five essays attempt to identify the Christian contributions to democratic life, those that are unrecognized as well as those that are identified, encouraged or resisted. In a democracy, Christians have rights to work for majority acceptance of their views equal to those of any other citizens, but such views are expounded not because they are Christian but because they contribute to human flourishing. Politics is the province of lay people rather than clerics, one good consequence of the separation of church and state.

Christians believe that God is a mystery of love, that the first two commandments require love of God and one another. Genuine love means that love has to be freely offered, and every good society works to provide an architecture of freedom. The rub comes with the claim that freedom can be found only in the truth. Freedom, reason, and love are a trinity, and this is one central reason why there is no case made, explicitly or covertly, for a theocracy.

The last five chapters outline something of the relationship between Christian truth and values in different areas of Western life.

While very few scientists are still confident that religion will wither away, the role of theology and metaphysics remains important in university life, as important as the continuing discussion of the compatibility of God and evolution, of the possibility or need of a Creator-Designer behind the design.

The rational case for God's existence needs to be made regularly, especially for reticent Catholics, even if the percentage of unbelievers has declined somewhat (at least in Australia), while differing views of marriage, family, and human life, often related to religious or irreligious worldviews, provoke crucial political conflict in the United States, Australia, and other places.

Finally, no discussion of religion and public life could avoid examining the foundations of human rights and the massive confusion on individual conscience, especially among Australian Catholics, which risks producing spectacular damage in Church and society.

Many have contributed to these essays, although the final product and any errors are my own. Particular thanks is due to Dr. Michael Casey for his input and editorial work and also to Professor Hayden Ramsay. Rob Dennis was assiduous in hunting down elusive references.

Christ himself told us "to render unto Caesar the things that are Caesar's and to God the things that are God's" (Lk 20:20–26). This remains the necessary starting point for any reflections on Christianity and political life.

—*George Cardinal Pell*
Sydney, October 2006

CATHOLICISM
& DEMOCRACY

1. LAW AND MORALITY

Whether and to what extent the principles of morality, and in particular religious morality, should be incorporated in the civil law is a difficult question, although for some it finds an apparently easy answer. Those who argue that religion and morality are private matters hold that they should not be incorporated into law at all. The usual justification for this position is that because each person comes by his own lights to his own estimation of the good, not only is general agreement on the principles of morality practically impossible, but the impossibility of general agreement powerfully suggests that there can be no general moral theory applicable to all.

It is certainly true that because the law must apply to everyone, it cannot be seen to "privilege" unjustly one moral system over another, and this applies especially to religious morality in an age when the number of practicing believers is declining in many Western countries. Given this, it seems merely a matter of common sense that religion and morality on the one hand, and law on the other, must be rigidly demarcated.

One problem with this is that common sense is never as simple as it appears to be, and often obscures beliefs and premises that are taken for granted. The assumption at work in the proposition that law and morality must always be separated has a comparatively short intellectual history. When this proposition first made its appearance it was highly controversial, and despite its assimilation into the academic and popular wisdom of our age it remains controversial still. The massive public scrutiny that is brought to bear on nominees for senior judicial appointment in the United

This chapter is an expanded version of a talk given to the Eggleston Society in Melbourne, Australia, 28 May 1997. Subsequently published in slightly modified form in the Pontifical Council for the Family's journal, *Familia et Vita* 10:3 (2005).

States and the growing criticism of "judicial activism" in other English-speaking countries such as the United Kingdom and Australia are indications of how controversial the "separation" of law and morality continues to be, especially in the area of jurisprudence. The morality that proponents of separation are particularly keen to exclude from the law is generally of course Christian morality. This term is understood very broadly to include not only expressly religious moral principles, such as those that trace the sanctity of life to its origins in a gift from God, but also moral principles drawn from traditions such as the natural law that uphold the sanctity of life and other key values on strictly philosophical grounds. Opponents of the natural law tradition view it, together with natural law principles still at work in civil law such as those supporting the marriage laws, as a disguised form of religious morality that has no place in modern secular law.[1] Underlying this opposition are certain assumptions about religion and reason being in exclusively antithetical relationship to each other and about religion upholding only strictly "religious" principles.

The sundering of religion and reason emerged clearly in the middle of the eighteenth century. Before that religion and reason were most often seen as compatible, even mutually necessary, not only in the Catholic tradition of thinking and theologizing but also in, for example, English thinking after Henry VIII.[2] Reason served man by deepening his understanding of God and the mysteries of

1. A classic and influential example of this view is John Rawls, *A Theory of Justice* (Cambridge, MA: Belknap Press, 1971). Martha Nussbaum is a leading contemporary exponent of this position: see for example Randall Baldwin Clark, "Platonic Love in a Colorado Court Room: Martha Nussbaum, John Finnis, and Plato's *Laws* in *Evans v. Romer*," *Yale Journal of Law and Humanities* 12 (2000): 1–38. For an analysis of this school of thought, see Robert P. George, "The Legal Enforcement of Morals," in *Making Men Moral: Civil Liberties and Public Morality* (Oxford: Clarendon Press, 1993).

2. For example, Richard Hooker (1554?–1600), one of the fathers of a distinctive Anglican theology, argues in *Laws of Ecclesiastical Polity* (1593) not only for the natural law but for a threefold approach to authority in religious matters, relying on reason, Scripture, and tradition—later known as "the three-legged stool." John Locke (1632–1704) in *An Essay Concerning Human Understanding* (1690), ed. Peter H. Nidditch (Oxford: Clarendon Press, 1975), writes:

both revelation and the created world. It was only in the eighteenth century that religion came to be seen by many as an impediment to the clear apprehension of the truth and that the explanations offered by reason came to be understood as destructive of the explanations offered by religion. From a situation where theology was queen of the sciences and reason's inspiration, religion became an elaborate system of superstition that clouded the understanding.

The historian Paul Johnson has identified the great Scottish historian and philosopher David Hume as "the first well-known European figure who not only proclaimed himself a genuine atheist in life, but died an atheist as well," which is undoubtedly the harder thing to do.[3] One small difficulty with this claim is that Hume was not an atheist. Perhaps it would be more accurate to say that though Hume produced batteries of argument against religious claims he never quite came to the point of an outright denial of God's existence.[4] For him, belief in God could not be proved, though such belief could be said to be psychologically and socially beneficial.[5] Hume did not believe in an afterlife, but on the question of an intelligent Creator perhaps we had better say he was—

Faith is nothing but a firm Assent of the Mind: which if it be regulated, as is our Duty, cannot be afforded to anything but upon good Reason; and so cannot be opposite to it. He that believes, without having any Reason for believing, may be in love with his own Fancies; but neither seeks Truth as he ought, nor pays the Obedience due his maker, who would have him use those discerning Faculties he has given him, to keep him out of mistake and errour (Book IV.17.24).

Chapter 18 of the same work goes into a detailed discussion of the relationship between faith and reason. Finally, Isaac Newton (1642–1727) in his General *Scholium* of the *Principia* (1687) and Robert Boyle (1627–92) in *The Excellence of Theology* (1674) are also two good examples of natural philosophers who presented a positive relationship between theology and natural philosophy.

3. Paul Johnson, *The Quest for God* (London: Harper Collins, 1996), 7.

4. See David Hume, *An Enquiry Concerning Human Understanding* (1748), in L. A. Selby-Bigge, ed., *Enquiries Concerning Human Understanding and Concerning the Principles of Morals* (1902), 3rd ed. rev. P. H. Nidditch (Oxford: Oxford University Press, 1975), Sections 10 and 11; and also David Hume, *Dialogues Concerning Natural Religion* (1779), ed. J. C. A. Gaskin (Oxford: Oxford University Press, 1993).

5. David Hume, "Natural History of Religion," in *Four Dissertations* (1757) (Bristol: Thoemmes Press, 1997).

just possibly—agnostic. Nevertheless, Hume's death in 1776 was seen by Benjamin Franklin as a portent, although Samuel Johnson could not be convinced that Hume felt no pain at the thought of complete annihilation.[6]

Over the century that followed in the wake of the Enlightenment and the French Revolution things moved quickly. Among the many important figures in late-eighteenth- and early-nineteenth-century intellectual life whose influence contributed to the secularization of the European mind, perhaps the most seminal was G. W. F. Hegel, especially through his influence on Karl Marx, who (drawing on the work of Ludwig Feuerbach)[7] turned Hegel's spiritualism upside down,[8] and even on Max Weber.[9] Although at times

---

6. Johnson, *The Quest for God*, 7.

7. On Feuerbach, see Eugene Kamenka, *The Philosophy of Ludwig Feuerbach* (London: Routledge and Kegan Paul, 1970).

8. For a useful summary of how Marx inverted Hegel's spiritualism, see Owen Chadwick, *The Secularization of the European Mind in the Nineteenth Century* (Cambridge: Cambridge University Press, 1975), 50–62. For a fuller explication of the thought of Marx and Hegel, see John Plamenatz, *Man and Society: A Critical Examination of Political Thought from Machiavelli to Marx*, vol. 3: *Hegel, Marx and the Idea of Progress* (New York: Longman, 1992).

9. Despite the similarities between Hegel and Weber, not many scholars have made a point of focusing on Hegel's influence on Weber. Hegel's influence was exerted indirectly through Marx, and because the Marx-Weber connection is much closer, there has been much more scholarly interest in it than in the Hegel-Weber connection. Some authors allude to Hegel's influence on Weber, or at least highlight similarities between them. See for example, E. B. F. Midgley, *The Ideology of Max Weber: A Thomist Critique* (Lanham, MD: Rowman and Littlefield, 1983), 42, 119–20. A more explicit statement on the Hegel-Weber connection is offered by Reinhard Bendix, *Max Weber: An Intellectual Portrait* (London: Methuen, 1966). Bendix observes, for example (at 387), that

> [Weber's] treatment of history as a causal succession of unique events, his emphasis on ideas in relation to action, his typological procedure, and, finally, his treatment of China and India, of charisma and tradition, as contrast-conceptions for the development of ethical rationalism and legal domination in Western Europe all reveal traces of Hegel's philosophy of history. Like Hegel, Weber insisted that nature consists of cyclical and repetitive events, whereas history is made up of non-repetitive acts. Not what people do but what they think about their actions is the proper subject of analysis. Every man is always both rational and passionate, never only one or the other; we must search out man's passion behind his reasoning and man's reasoning behind his passions.

religiously orthodox, Hegel propounded a view of human history as "an inexorable progression from lower to higher forms, from ignorance to knowledge, from unreason to reason." Hegel held that in this process religion has an important place, but one that must be ultimately superseded by higher forms of consciousness.[10]

The notion that belief in God is part of a lower phase in human development took a tremendous hold on the Western mind. Paul Johnson claims it "penetrated every aspect of intellectual life, from the physical sciences to the burgeoning social sciences such as philology, economics, sociology and history, and even biblical studies."[11] This development was accompanied by certain scientific breakthroughs that seemed to undermine further the foundations of religion and morality. In the 1820s and 1830s the world's geology was totally recast to undermine fatally the traditional chronology and historicity of the Old Testament. This was followed by the Darwinian revolution in the 1840s and 1850s, which totally demolished the scientific authority of the book of Genesis as it had previously been understood by many believers.

In 1860 Thomas Huxley, Darwin's most fanatical devotee, famously debated Samuel Wilberforce, the Anglican bishop of Oxford, on evolution at the annual meeting of the British Association for the Advancement of Science, virtually declaring "intellectual war on Christianity" in the process. "Thereafter it became almost a commonplace, in intellectual circles, to assume that religious belief was a receding force in human spirituality, and this applied whether you valued or despised it."[12] Sigmund Freud provided a means of reinforcing and extending this view when he published *The Interpretation of Dreams* in 1899, laying out the basis of psychoanalysis's powerfully disenchanting approach to human nature. Committed to the advancement of an expressly atheistic understanding of reason, Darwin, Marx, and Freud were to become the three most

10. Johnson, *The Quest for God*, 7–8.
11. Ibid.
12. Ibid., 8–9. For an account of Huxley's debate with Wilberforce, see Rodney Stark, *For the Glory of God* (Princeton, NJ: Princeton University Press, 2003), 185–92.

powerful intellectual forces in the first half of the twentieth century. Darwin alone among these nineteenth-century idols remains to continue this project today.

Matthew Arnold's oft-quoted lines from his 1867 poem "Dover Beach" offer an accurate and powerful presentation of the prevailing sentiment of his time. Arnold wrote that "the sea of Faith"

> Was once too, at the full, and round earth's shore
> Lay like the folds of a bright girdle furl'd.
> But now I only hear
> Its melancholy, long, withdrawing roar,
> Retreating, to the breath
> Of the night-wind, down the vast edges drear
> And naked shingles of the world.

Others were not so elegiac. The German philosopher Friedrich Nietzsche shared nothing of Arnold's romantically expressed sense of loss. "God is dead! God remains dead! And we have killed him!" he famously wrote in 1882.[13] Nietzsche had scathing contempt for the English utilitarians and rationalists, holding that they did not go far enough. They had renounced the Christian religion but did not dare to renounce the morality of Christianity, which continued to hold sway in secularized form despite the death of God. "For the English," Nietzsche wrote, "morality is not a problem yet."[14] A generation or two would have to pass before it became so.

The twentieth century was an unimaginable catastrophe. Technological progress, one of the great blessings of the period, has massively extended the capacity of tyrants to kill. Between 85 and 100 million people were killed by Communist regimes alone,[15] and

---

13. Friedrich Nietzsche, *The Gay Science* (1882), ed. Bernard Williams, trans. Josefine Nauckhoff and Adrian Del Caro (Cambridge: Cambridge University Press, 2001), 120.

14. Friedrich Nietzsche, *Twilight of the Idols* (1889), in *The Anti-Christ, Ecce Homo, Twilight of the Idols and Other Writings*, ed. Aaron Ridley and Judith Norman, trans. Judith Norman (Cambridge: Cambridge University Press, 2005), 194.

15. See the estimates detailed by contributors to Stéphane Courtois, Nicolas

another 21 million were killed by the German National Socialists. According to one estimate, perhaps as many as 170 million have been killed by state-sponsored violence to 1993, more than four times the number of those killed in battle in local and international wars since 1900.[16] Three of the four most murderous regimes, those of Lenin and Stalin, Mao, and Pol Pot, openly proclaimed atheist materialism, while Hitler's regime was avowedly pagan. All four tyrannies were radically opposed to religion, morality, and law.

We should be very cautious about attributing the crimes of these regimes directly to the ideas of the Enlightenment, although we are on safer ground in drawing a link to the worst practices of the French Revolution, particularly in the use made of law to authorize terror and mass murder. There is no doubt, however, that the great totalitarianisms of the twentieth century shared some of the foundational presuppositions of the secularism that Enlightenment thought promoted. Totalitarianism held religion in contempt, seeing it as a source of weakness and superstition. It might be manipulated for short-term political advantage if necessary, but the morality that upheld the value of human life, and insisted on respect for the weak—unborn children, the disabled and mentally handicapped, the old and sick—was always regarded as a deficient point of view, the perspective of "decadent" bourgeois democratic societies.

This contempt for morality and religion led to a particular approach to the law. The totalitarian regimes mocked law and the rule of law, enacting legislation enshrining extensive rights and protections while ruling through terror administered by pseudo-legal procedures. It was no accident that the law was degraded in this way as religion and morality were attacked and undermined.

Nor should it be assumed that this sort of logic unfolds only

---

Werth, Jean-Louis Panné, Andrzej Paczkowski, Karel Bartosek, and Jean-Louis Margolin, *The Black Book of Communism* (1997), ed. Mark Kramer, trans. Jonathan Murphy (Cambridge, MA: Harvard University Press, 1999).

16. Rudolph J. Rummel, *Death by Government* (New Brunswick, NJ: Transaction, 1994).

in totalitarian dictatorships. Pope John Paul II in his 1995 encyclical *Evangelium vitae* warned that when "the original and inalienable right to life is questioned or denied on the basis of a parliamentary vote or the will of one part of the people—even if it is a majority," the right to life ceases to be a right based on "the inviolable dignity of the person, but is made subject to the will of the stronger part." A society that takes to itself the power to determine who does and does not enjoy a right to life is no longer "a common home" for all. The apparent legality of its processes and decisions in this regard is a betrayal of legality, for unless the democratic ideal "acknowledges and safeguards the dignity of every human person, [it] is betrayed in its very foundations." For a state to recognize in law a "right" to infanticide and euthanasia is to "attribute to human freedom a perverse and evil significance: that of an absolute power over others and against others. This is the death of true freedom."[17]

Abortion and euthanasia are at the center of arguments about the relationship between religion, morality, and law. Supporters of abortion and euthanasia "rights" regularly describe (or deride) opposing principles as "religious" in an attempt to disqualify them from being taken into consideration by legislators and jurists. A related argument tells opponents they have no right to "impose" their personal moral views on the community as a whole. Notoriously, this particular argument is also offered by legislators who want both to retain the support of a traditional constituency and to support bad laws.

Both arguments are deeply problematic. The suggestion that religious views should be silenced or that believers should be excluded from taking part in public debate cannot be accepted in a democracy. Religious people have as much right as the nonreligious to state their views and to argue for them. The argument that personal moral views should not be imposed on others when it comes to lawmaking is incoherent and misleading. It is incoher-

17. John Paul II, Encyclical Letter *Evangelium vitae* (1995), §20.

ent because a great deal of law implicitly "imposes" a particular moral view on the wider society. It would be disingenuous to pretend that the legalization of abortion on demand or euthanasia does not impose a certain moral view on the rest of society. This is especially true when arguments for abortion and euthanasia are based on rights. The appeal to rights is a moral argument, and it is this appeal to moral authority that gives force to laws enshrining rights.

The argument about imposing personal morality is also misleading, and this is perhaps the more important criticism to make, especially from the practical perspective of those actively involved in the defense of life in the public square. In the passage from *Evangelium vitae* quoted above John Paul II does not invoke the law of God or the Ten Commandments as reasons for opposing attacks on life, although elsewhere in the encyclical these explicitly religious and Christian grounds for opposition are set out at length.[18] Instead he bases this opposition on "the inviolable dignity of the person," the concept on which most mainline theories of rights also base themselves. Is defending life on the basis of the inviolable dignity of the person really the same thing as imposing one's personal moral views on the rest of the community?

If it is, then the same must hold for laws against genocide and slavery and unjust discrimination, which are also based on the inviolable dignity of the person. If opposition to abortion or euthanasia is no more than a "personal" matter, a product of idiosyncratic religious or moral beliefs, then so too is opposition to slavery and genocide. It is an interesting indication of the depths of our confusion that while a legislator who was personally opposed to the legalization of slavery but voted for it anyway would be regarded as a humbug, a legislator who does the same thing on abortion is treated as a moral hero.

In this confusion we begin to see what lies behind John Paul II's startling warning about democracy "effectively mov[ing] to-

18. See, for example, ibid., §§7–10.

wards a form of totalitarianism." It begins to happen at a practical level when we simultaneously hold that rights which arise from the dignity of the person are also a matter of "bargaining." New rights can be claimed or created, and whatever privileges can be negotiated around them are then secured by reference to human dignity, even when these new rights are directly contrary to the human dignity of some, for example, the unborn or the elderly sick. This confusion about the nature of rights debases their currency and undermines the first principles of democracy. Such freedom gradually becomes a tyrannical "freedom of the 'the strong' against the weak, who have no choice but to submit."[19]

The confusion about rights in democratic societies stems from a fundamental confusion about freedom. As Pope John Paul emphasizes in *Evangelium vitae,* the prevailing concept of democratic freedom is radically individualistic, "exalt[ing] the isolated individual in an absolute way," giving "no place to solidarity, to openness to others and service of them."[20] Coupled with this idea of freedom as absolute autonomy is the fading of the notion of universal moral principles and the decline of binding moral truths. "Freedom negates and destroys itself, and becomes a factor leading to the destruction of others, when it no longer recognizes and respects its essential link with the truth."[21] If each individual becomes "the sole and indisputable point of reference for his own choices, [not] the truth about good and evil, but only his subjective and changeable opinion," interest, or whim, "social life ventures on to the shifting sands of complete relativism."[22] As agreement on foundational moral principles is taken to be impossible, majority votes and the decisions of judges determine contentious issues absolutely. This is not a sufficient basis on which to safeguard the long-term public legitimacy of the law.

One function of law is to defend the key values of human society, as well as human persons. But relativism is powerfully cor-

---

19. Ibid., §§19–20.
21. Ibid.

20. Ibid., §19.
22. Ibid., §§19–20.

rupting, not least when it is enshrined in the law itself. Again, the situation is confused and confusing. On the one hand, it is claimed that consensus on moral questions is impossible because moral values are relative and should not be imposed on others. At the same time, however, a certain moral vision is introduced to the law, primarily by removing legal constraints or prohibitions in areas around sexuality and the sanctity of life. This is justified by invoking civil rights or the need to defend human dignity, especially in light of the experience of totalitarianism, and particularly Nazism. Those who seek to oppose these innovations are told they are imposing their morality on others, while those who pursue new "rights" impose them on society in the name of freedom and human dignity. Relativism is at once asserted (to disarm critics) and denied (to secure new principles as rights) in a process that often resembles a play for power rather than a genuine deliberative process.

In this way the insistence that morality must be excluded from the law leads to the law's deformation. Instead of protecting life and critical social values, law begins to undermine them. In the process the authority of law and the legitimacy of the lawmaking process come into question. *Evangelium vitae* attracted considerable attention at the time of its publication for its restatement of traditional Catholic teaching on unjust laws and "the necessary *conformity of civil law with the moral law.*"[23] Pope John Paul quotes St. Thomas Aquinas's teaching that "[e]very law made by man can be called a law insofar as it derives from the natural law. But if it is somehow opposed to the natural law, then it is not really a law but rather a corruption of the law."[24]

Law exists to protect the good of the individual and the common good. This is the basis of its legitimacy and authority. The right to life is fundamental. There can be no rights unless this right is protected and respected. Because laws permitting abortion and

23. Ibid., §72.
24. St. Thomas Aquinas, *Summa theologiae* (1–2, 95, 2). Quoted at ibid.

euthanasia are utterly at odds with both the common good and human rights, they cannot be "morally binding law." The obligation concerning these laws is not one of obedience but of conscientious objection.[25]

Questions of life and death throw these considerations into stark relief. On other matters things may not always be so clear. For example: to what extent should there be conformity between the moral law and civil law in the area of sexual behavior and family formation? The teaching of the Second Vatican Council in *Gaudium et spes* is an important foundation here: "civil authority should consider it a sacred duty to acknowledge the true nature of marriage and the family, to protect and foster them, to safeguard public morality and promote domestic prosperity."[26]

What does it mean for the law to "protect and foster" marriage and family life and to "safeguard public morality"? Professor John Finnis has argued that in modern legal theory and practice a distinction is made between the supervision of "truly private adult consensual conduct," which is now considered "to be outside the state's normally proper role," and the supervision of the public realm, or "the moral-cultural-educational environment"[27]—what Michael Novak has called the "moral ecology" of a society.[28] Although the traditional view that "the state should encourage true worth and discourage immorality" is "now judged to be mistaken," the supervision of "the *public realm or environment*" is still a very important part of the state's justification for claiming the loyalty of its citizens. This is the environment in which young people are educated and all citizens are helped or hindered in being self-controlled persons "rather than slaves to impulse or sensual gratification."[29]

25. *Evangelium vitae*, §§72–73.

26. Second Vatican Council, Pastoral Constitution on the Church in the Modern World, *Gaudium et spes* (1965), §52.

27. John M. Finnis, "Law, Morality, and 'Sexual Orientation,'" *Notre Dame Law Review* 69 (1994): 1049–76, at 1052.

28. Michael Novak, *On Cultivating Liberty: Reflections on Moral Ecology* (Lanham MD: Rowman and Littlefield, 1999).

29. Finnis, "Law, Morality, and 'Sexual Orientation,'" 1052–53.

The "normalization" of homosexuality has substantially eroded the capacity of the civil law to cultivate or protect the moral ecology of society. As Finnis explains, often this followed from measures to protect homosexuals from discrimination on the grounds of their sexual orientation. With the passage of such laws discrimination as such very quickly ceased to be the issue, and these laws were used by activists as means of "extending full legal protection to *public* activities intended specifically to promote, procure and facilitate homosexual *conduct.*" It was soon understood, Finnis says, that

the adoption of a law framed to prohibit "discrimination on the grounds of sexual orientation" would require the prompt abandonment of all attempts by the political community to discourage homosexual conduct by means of educational policies, restrictions on prostitution, non-recognition of homosexual "marriages" and adoptions, and so forth. It is judged (and in my view soundly) that the law itself would perforce have changed from teaching, in many ways, that homosexual conduct is bad to teaching, massively, that it is a type of sexual activity as good as any other (and per se much less involved with onerous responsibilities than is the sexual union of husband and wife or, in perhaps other ways, the life of those who live in unmarried chastity).[30]

These changes are socially disastrous. But in a democracy, while we are entitled to explain the religious basis of our views on these matter, the greater challenge is to explain in human, nonreligious terms why the protection of the moral ecology is necessary and important for society. Often these explanations will be cast in instrumental or utilitarian terms, focusing on the unfortunate social consequences of particular developments. These explanations can be very compelling, particularly when they draw on the massed empirical findings of studies into the personal and social consequences of marriage and family breakdown, abortion, legalized pornography and prostitution, and drug addiction. But they have two particular weaknesses.

30. Ibid., 1054–55.

The first weakness is that the strength of an argument from empirical data can be vitiated by drawing attention to exceptions. Exceptions, of course, do not disprove a general conclusion, but in discussion in the public square they can have a disproportionate effect in blunting an argument. For example, it is not uncommon for the media to respond to yet more research showing that in general families based on marriage ensure the best outcomes for children by generating sentimental profiles of other family types who have achieved good outcomes for their children despite hardship, discrimination, and so on.

The second weakness is that empirical arguments do not take us beyond what works and what does not. They still leave us with the task of explaining the underlying moral or metaphysical reality behind the benefits or the harms that they identify. For example, the detailed evidence of the harmfulness of pornography still requires us to explain why it is wrong and why as a society we should be concerned when individuals harm themselves through using it, even if this does not lead to others being harmed.

Pointing out the weaknesses of empirical arguments is not to suggest that we should not make the fullest use possible of empirical studies and their findings. But we cannot rely on these sorts of arguments and data exclusively. We also need to offer clear explanations for the values that support life and human flourishing, and the reasons why the law and the wider culture should protect and foster these values. The works of Professor Finnis and others, such as Professor Robert George,[31] offer us exemplary models for how this might be done, as does the teaching of Pope John Paul II in his major encyclicals such as *Evangelium vitae, Veritatis splendor,* and *Centesimus annus.*

The determined lobbies that push various "liberation agendas" exploit the confusion in the public mind about private and public morality, and are particularly adept at intimidating politicians with this confusion. The responsibility of the state to "iden-

---

31. George, *Making Men Moral.*

tify, encourage, facilitate and support the truly worthwhile (including moral virtue)" and to "discourage and hinder the harmful and evil" is treated as being equivalent to the state's using criminal sanctions against private and consensual acts between adults.[32] In this way, the proper instinct for the law not to intrude into private lives is used to distort the relationship between law and morality and to change the entire public environment, particularly that surrounding marriage and the raising of children.

Here we are confronted again with the fundamental problem of what Michael Novak calls "vulgar relativism" or "nihilism with a happy face." For those who adhere to this, "it is certain that there is no truth, only opinion: *my* opinion, *your* opinion."[33] Novak argues that one of the lessons of the twentieth century is that "truth matters." In the light of this lesson, the most perilous threat to a free society is "the poisonous, corrupting culture of relativism," particularly when it comes to the education of the young:

"There is no such thing as truth," they teach even the little ones. "Truth is bondage. Believe what seems right to you. There are as many truths as there are individuals. Follow your feelings. Do as you please. Get in touch with yourself. Do what feels comfortable." Those who speak in this way prepare the jails of the twenty-first century. They do the work of tyrants.[34]

Novak argues that the free society is moral or it is not a free society at all. I believe he is right. In 1986 the Congregation for the Doctrine of the Faith pointed out that when moral considerations are removed from the law, and specifically when civil legislation protects behavior to which no one has a right (even though the law might appropriately leave such activity alone), then no one should be surprised when other distorted notions and practices gain ground.[35] These include distorted notions of freedom that

32. Finnis, "Law, Morality, and 'Sexual Orientation,'" 1076.

33. Michael Novak, "Awakening from Nihilism: The Templeton Prize Address," *First Things* 45 (August–September 1994): 18–22, at 20.

34. Ibid., 21.

35. Congregation for the Doctrine of the Faith, "Letter to the Bishops of the Catholic Church on the Pastoral Care of Homosexual Persons" (1986), §10.

are inimical to the stability and endurance of democratic societies.

While democratic societies remain democratic, opportunities remain open to us, and we should not be shy in taking them up. Those who value life and consider the family the best available institution for ensuring the happiness of parents and the best possible source of love and care for children need to put their moral principles into terms that others can understand and to facilitate as much public discussion about these matters as possible. The law needs a moral compass to ensure that it serves rather than dominates society. Restoring this compass to the law is primarily a work of persuasion, and this itself is a moral task. It requires us to respect other people's freedom, to engage in dialogue with them, to create trust and friendship, and in this way to secure majority support for democratic decision that brings the law back into the service of the common good.

2. THE CHURCH AND POLITICS

Much ink has been spilled on the relationship of religion and politics. Unfortunately there will be no breakthroughs here, only my attempt to identify some markers in this often vexed discussion and to discuss a few particular problems.

Our Lord's teachings have profound consequences for public life, but Jesus never (or hardly ever) delivered a political sermon. Demonstrably, Christ was not a social activist; but demonstrably, the Gospel is deeply subversive of all politics, proclaiming new attitudes to power, wealth, opportunity, and government. Christ was concerned first and foremost with God's love and mercy for us, with the imperative of personal conversion of heart to faith and goodness, and long-term consequences of our actions for ourselves and others. This long-term view included life beyond the grave and the reward and punishment that lie there for us.

The first post or marker is Christ's injunction "render unto Caesar the things that are Caesar's and to God the things that are God's."[1] Caesar and God parallel the Gospel contrast between the Heavenly Kingdom and the powers of the world. Christ is not calling us to abandon either one, but is clear that we can properly render to Caesar what is Caesar's only if we render to God what is God's, and vice versa. Good citizenship requires people to be virtuous, and it is a great help to this if they are also God-fearing.

Palestine was a political hotbed in Our Lord's time, the Northern Ireland of the Roman Empire, but Christ endorsed no political faction and outlined no political program. He escaped when some wanted to make him a political leader,[2] and he certainly did not endorse political violence, although one of his apostles was Si-

This chapter was originally an address to the Institute of Public Affairs, Melbourne, Australia, 17 November 1999.
1. Lk. 20:20–26.   2. Jn. 6:4–15.

mon the Zealot.[3] He said little directly about the proper exercise of authority and power, but by word and deed he emphasized the importance of service.[4] His models were not the power brokers of this world, successful or unsuccessful, but little children.[5] Christ's kingdom goes far beyond this world.[6]

The second marker is found in the Second Vatican Council's Pastoral Constitution on the Church and in the Modern World, *Gaudium et spes* (1965). In this document the council fathers emphasize that it is the duty of the lay members of the Church to face into the world and into society. From the Catholic perspective public life is primarily the responsibility of lay people rather than clergy or members of religious orders. It is lay people—not exclusively, but generally—who should take up the work of advocacy and day-to-day politics.[7] This is especially true in developed societies where levels of education for lay people are very high, unlike, for example, developing countries such as Papua New Guinea, where in 2004 Archbishop Barnes of Port Moresby made a major public intervention against government corruption that was instrumental in bringing about a change of government.

Lay people are powerfully assisted in this work by the social teaching of the Church and the political ethics that it has developed over centuries. Most people are little aware of the influence of Catholic teaching in social and political thinking, but without this the United Nations Charter, the United States' Constitution and many others, and the common law tradition would be very different from their present forms.[8]

3. Lk. 6:15.   4. See, for example, Jn. 13:3–15.
5. Mt. 18:1–5.   6. Cf. Jn. 18:33–38.
7. Second Vatican Council, Pastoral Constitution on the Church in the Modern World, *Gaudium et spes* (1965), §43.
8. On the influence of Catholic political and social teaching: on the United Nations Charter, see Mary Ann Glendon, *A World Made New: Eleanor Roosevelt and the Universal Declaration of Human Rights* (New York: Random House, 2001); on the U.S. Constitution, see especially John Courtney Murray, S.J., *We Hold These Truths: Catholic Reflections on the American Proposition* (Kansas City, MO: Sheed and Ward, 1960), and also E. S. Corwin, "The 'Higher Law' Background of American Constitutional Law" and

A third marker is required by the nature of contemporary Western society, where many believe that economic reforms are the key to social, political, and intellectual changes, that modern societies are secular and materialistic, and that the pursuit of wealth has replaced belief as the cement of society. In our enthusiasm to participate in the public debate, in our haste to make religion appear relevant, in the weakness of our faith, we can unconsciously adopt these premises, or talk as though we do. Christians cannot engage in politics in the way the powers of the world do. A church that cannot see beyond the ideologies of the age is not a prophetic church.

As long ago as 1975 an ecumenical group of theologians in the United States drafted an "Appeal for Theological Affirmation," known as the Hartford Appeal after the city in Connecticut where the document was prepared. The Appeal strongly endorsed the importance of work for justice and the poor but deplored the tendency to equate the kingdom of God with the results of human efforts to build a just society.

One of the drafters and signatories of the Hartford Appeal, Cardinal Avery Dulles, S.J., spelled this out further. In our social justice statements, he urged, we must not unwittingly give the impression that what is truly important is "not the faith and holiness that leads to everlasting life but rather the structuring of human society." If in our sociopolitical analysis there is a total lack of eschatological reference, we can seem to have little confidence in our spiritual patrimony and be suggesting that the Church is a this-world "satellite institution revolving around the primary world of industry and government."[9]

This is a particular danger in Western countries, where the

"The Debt of American Constitutional Law to Natural Law Concepts," in *Corwin on the Constitution*, ed. Richard Loss (Cornell University Press: London, 1981); and on the development of Western law, see Harold J. Berman, *Law and Revolution: The Formation of the Western Legal Tradition* (Cambridge, MA: Harvard University Press, 1983).

9. Avery Dulles, S.J., *The Reshaping of Catholicism* (San Francisco: Harper and Row, 1988), 176–77.

number of people professing no religion has increased from the early 1960s, sometimes dramatically.[10] One temptation in this situation is to remove the vertical dimension of religion altogether and to concentrate largely on social justice and political questions. The supernatural dimension is not so much denounced as ignored. This was one of the dangers of liberation theology, which Pope John Paul II successfully opposed in South America.[11]

Because the Church is not primarily a political organization it does not have to have a view on many or most political questions. Church leaders can and sometimes should speak publicly where there are clear issues of public morality. While the Church leadership must concentrate on unity in essential matters of faith and morals, they are less concerned that there should be a single church view on many political questions. Rather, the key point for church leaders is to encourage people to see how serious the political process is, to form a vision, to contribute regularly, not to be apathetic.

For example, if a country is reforming its system of taxation, unanimity among Catholics is not required when it comes to assessing the merits or shortcomings of a particular reform proposal. It is not the role of bishops or even church agencies to enunciate a "church line" on something like tax reform. An issue like this

10. The Center for the Study of Global Christianity's *World Christian Database* (www.worldchristiandatabase.org) estimates that the percentage of those professing no religion has risen in the United States from just under 2 percent in 1900 to 4.8 percent in 1970, and to 9.26 percent in 2005. In Australia the figures are 1 percent in 1900, rising to 4.5 percent in 1970, and to a little over 15 percent in 2005 (down from 16.6 percent in 1996). In Europe, less than 0.4 percent were nonreligious in 1900, but by 1970 this figure had risen to 13 percent, and to just under 15 percent by 2005. Globally, however, the number of people professing no religion is falling. The figure rose from 0.19 percent in 1900 to just under 14.5 percent in 1970, thereafter falling to about 12.5 percent in 2000, and to 11.9 percent in 2005.

11. The key documents of John Paul II's pontificate on liberation theology were the two Instructions *Libertatis nuntius* ("On Certain Aspects of the 'Theology of Liberation'"), 1984, and *Libertatis conscientia* ("On Christian Freedom and Liberation"), 1986, issued by the Congregation for the Doctrine of the Faith. For an account of John Paul II's response to liberation theology, see George Weigel, *Witness to Hope: The Biography of Pope John Paul II* (New York: Harper Collins, 1999), chapter 8.

is complicated, involving both short-term and long-term issues of importance to the common good. Issues to be taken into consideration would include fairness, the intended or unintended consequences for families or for business and investment, and the importance of ensuring that government has a solid base to finance welfare and social services, both now and into the future.

When this issue arose in Australia some years ago, the Catholic bishops put forward ten principles on tax reform for all the participants in the debate to consider. Catholics were free to reject or accept them and have different views, while still accepting the Ten Commandments, the Beatitudes, and the basic concepts of natural law.

There are some within the Church, of course, who disagree with this approach. These people prefer a model where an agency is authorized to provide "guidance" on how to apply principles enunciated by the bishops, arguing that without such guidance ordinary Catholics are hard-pressed to come to an informed assessment of their own on difficult political and social questions. This is not an approach I favor. When no basic questions of faith and morals are at stake, a certain level of confidence in the ability of Catholics to think for themselves is appropriate, perhaps even necessary.

A second question is whether the Church should cooperate with the state in some harm-minimization programs. Should Catholic hospitals provide injecting rooms for heroin addicts? Should the Church provide condoms in her parishes, youth centers, and schools to help curtail disease and prevent pregnancies? Should the Church provide information to young and old on "safer" forms of homosexual activity? Should Church agencies provide advice on who are reputable abortionists, or provide facilities for abortions so that there would be fewer health risks to mothers? Less plausibly, should beer be sold in school canteens to distract teenagers from spirits and drugs? Should schools provide cigarette holders and low-strength cigarettes to decrease health risks for young smokers?

We began by remarking on the distinction between what be-

longs to Caesar and what belongs to God. "The children of this
world"[12] often think and act differently from those with a strongly
religious and Christian orientation, sometimes starting their moral
reasoning from a different set of premises and using principles of
compromise, consensus, and calculation rather than moral principles. There is a perennial temptation to think in these ways, and
the danger is increased if one is uncertain about what is distinctive
about Christian morality and if one knows no moral philosophy,
let alone moral theology. A surprising number of well-educated
people can and do dismiss the entire project of Catholic ethics
and moral theology without the encumbrance of any knowledge
of what they are dismissing.

Every religion, including Catholicism (and all Christianity
when it has not been liberalized beyond recognition), has a couple
of key moral tasks: firstly to present principles, norms, and ideals
that we should attempt to follow; and secondly to provide struc-
tures for coping with human weakness through forgiveness and the
call to conversion, again and again.

Christ did not go around urging people to be careful if they
cannot manage to be good. He had a stronger belief in the human
potential. Nor did he go around handing out condoms and syring-
es, literally or metaphorically. He had greater confidence in weak
and foolish humanity.

Our society needs the Christian churches to remember their
Master's teachings. There is no point to a church that is not in
some way countercultural, that does not point beyond the next
moment, beyond a short-term compassion. Christ's compassion
is not an urgent, explosive feeling but an ethical compassion: he
forgave those he judged truly repentant, and expected much of
those who received his forgiveness.[13] He embraced the little children and fed the hungry, but did not let them leave before he had
also shown them something of his truth.[14]

12. Lk. 16:8.   13. Mt. 18: 24–35.
14. Mk. 10:13–16 and Mt. 15:29–39.

Catholics acknowledge that the role of a government and government agencies is different from the role of a church, just as Catholics acknowledge that not every immoral activity should be illegal. Nevertheless, although not all immoral activities should be illegal, it does not follow that all legal activities are thereby moral. The Church's ethic is not one of harm-minimization and acceptance of wrongdoing. For example, drug abuse is a scourge. Present measures are not working, and no quick, easy solutions are at hand. Certainly more facilities for those willing to enter detoxification and rehabilitation programs are needed. This is surely a better, though harder, approach than injecting rooms. It is also more congruent with the ethic of life-affirming service the Church preaches and with her vision of the moral life as seeking genuine human fulfillment and happiness in this life and, please God, in the life to come.

My final problem area concerns the form of democratic government. Should a democracy such as Australia, for example, retain its links to the British monarchy or become a republic?

Provided that whatever system of government chosen is substantially and genuinely democratic, no clear-cut moral objections to either option are entailed. The important thing here for clergy speaking on this matter is to make it clear that private conscience has an unfettered choice between the options. A well-formed conscience could vote either way.

This question was the subject of a Constitutional Convention in Australia in 1998, at which there were at least five members of the clergy representing both sides of the debate (and one abstention). There was no objection to this, reflecting that clergy are citizens, with a right to speak, while those listening have every right to accept or reject their point of view.

Of course some people did object to the particular positions that these members of the clergy took on this question, and on the subsequent referendum. This reminds me of the comment of the late archbishop of Melbourne, Archbishop Daniel Mannix, who wryly observed that people never object to clergy intervening in politics provided they do so on their side. Perhaps the Church just cannot win here: if she becomes too involved in the large questions of the day she is accused of being too political; if she ignores them, she is accused of neglect and indifference.

The system of democratic government that a society should adopt is not a party political question. It is a political issue of a particular type. I am almost tempted to say it is a pre-political question, because it involves questions of national identity and self-understanding unique to whatever country in which they may arise. As I said earlier, without the Catholic Church's natural law and faith ethic many constitutions would have a different form. Constitutional issues call for a renewed interest in politics, for the Church too. Even in good times a nation needs to be interested in more than bread and butter issues. Without ideals, and long-term commitment to these ideals, a nation atrophies. Constitutional debate focuses our minds on these questions, and on what a country stands for and values.

It is on the question of a country's values that the Church has a particularly important role to play. To put this question another way, what are the sources of a secular society's values? Can it be taken for granted that Westerners will always be committed to human rights and concern for the poor? Or does the commitment to these values need to be renewed with each generation? If so, where does the energy needed for this renewal come from? How do we get young people to take these values seriously and make a personal commitment to them? And what sustains this commitment against the powerful appeals of individualism and consumerism and the fantastic rewards that come with material success for the lucky few?

It is easy to assume that people will always give to the poor and be concerned about social justice. But this does not happen by itself. Many great civilizations have shown no regard for these values at all and have even considered them weaknesses. The civilization of Rome at the advent of Christianity is a major example. In countries such as Australia governments are increasingly concerned about the decline in philanthropic giving, and many ordinary Australians worry that our egalitarian ethos is being eroded by the scramble to succeed.

Religion provides an important corrective to these trends. Every society requires a goodly percentage of active believers to ensure that the values of a fair go and respect for others are promoted, and passed on to the next generation. The sort of values that are essential for a decent, prosperous, and stable society can be outlined in a constitution, but to give them life and to strengthen them among people, especially the young, secularism is not enough.

Passion is what is required, not in the sense Georg Simmel described as "sterile excitation," but in the sense of a drive that compels us to the consistent service of the common good. Max Weber, not always an infallible guide to either religion or politics, understood something about passion, distinguishing it from the compulsive agitation "running into emptiness devoid of all feeling of objective responsibility" that is so abundant in modern life, and especially in modern politics, and that is often taken to be what passion means. Genuine passion, especially in politics, requires a sense of proportion, a capacity for responsibility, and the ability to engage with reality "with inner concentration and calmness."[15] In its etymology the word *passion* goes back to the Latin verb "to suffer," and a capacity if not quite to suffer then certainly to work long, hard, and without thanks for the good is undoubtedly a part of what genuine passion in politics and public life means.

The sources of passion and conviction are not exclusively religious, although it might be said of some of the nonreligious sources that they draw on a displaced religious impulse: think of the religious zeal that supporters bring to causes and parties such as the Greens. The critical point, however, is that secular politics

15. Max Weber, "Politics as a Vocation" (1919), in *From Max Weber: Essays in Sociology*, ed. and trans. H. H. Gerth and C. Wright Mills (London: Routledge and Kegan Paul, 1948), 115–16. The reference to Simmel is Weber's and is taken from these pages.

needs a healthy balance of religious capital to draw on, both to sustain the values that are essential to a free and prosperous society and to engender a personal commitment to these values on the part of its citizens. All sorts of distortions follow when this capital is run down or taken into overdraft. But that is the subject for another occasion.

3. CATHOLICISM & THE ARCHITECTURE OF FREEDOM

In 1894 the English prime minister Lord Rosebery appointed to the universities of Oxford and Cambridge Regius Professors of Modern History, neither of whom had published a book or would do so in their lifetimes. The first of these was Rosebery's old tutor at Oxford, Frederick Powell. The other had been debarred from entering Cambridge in 1850 by the unrepealed religious tests against Catholics. His name was John Emerich Edward Dalberg-Acton, better known to us as Lord Acton.

Acton was a man of immense erudition, who became an inspiring public speaker. He is remembered today primarily for his aphorism that "power tends to corrupt and absolute power corrupts absolutely"; changed by a contemporary cynic into "power corrupts and the loss of power corrupts absolutely." Even amongst churchmen his influence has been significant. In September 1964, as a student in Rome during the third session of the Second Vatican Council, I remember Cardinal Cushing of Boston reminding the council fathers of Acton's claim that "freedom is the highest political end," a sentiment that the council partly endorsed in its Declaration on Religious Freedom, *Dignitatas humanae* (1965). It is a pity that his great project for a universal history of liberty never eventuated.

Acton was born in 1834 into an old landed family of English Catholic recusants. His studies in France, Germany, and Scotland, as well as England, helped him become a cosmopolitan figure, con-

This chapter was originally the inaugural Acton Lecture on Religion and Freedom, delivered at the Centre for Independent Studies, Sydney, Australia, 4 August 1999, and shortly thereafter published by the Centre of Independent Studies as an occasional paper.

servative and aristocratic in temper, although a liberal rather than a Tory in politics. A largely silent member of the House of Commons for the Whigs for six years (1859–64), he was a trusted adviser to the liberal prime minister William Gladstone. Acton drew his political philosophy from Edmund Burke, believing firmly in the importance of custom, tradition, and what we today would call civil society or social capital as the guarantee and "organic foundation" of individual freedom against the power of the state.

Throughout his life Acton was a devout Catholic, while skeptical and often critical. He believed that faith had nothing to fear from history, and that Catholicism was by nature liberal rather than clerical and obscurantist. This outlook ran counter to the Catholic spirit of his times. The restoration of the Catholic hierarchy to England in 1850 reinforced an ultramontanism there that was at once triumphalist and defensive, and sometimes narrow and ungenerous in intellectual and theological matters. This was compounded by international developments that saw the end of the temporal power of the pope over the Papal States, the declaration of the First Vatican Council concerning papal infallibility in 1870, and the publication of Pius IX's *Syllabus* of eighty errors (1864), including condemnations of the separation of church and state, religious freedom, and the proposition that the Roman Pontiff should reconcile himself with progress, liberalism, and contemporary political life *(civilitas)*. It was not a good time for Catholic liberals.

Acton sought to apply to the story of the Church the critical historical scholarship he had learned in Germany, and he held firmly to the view that the Catholic scholar should be free to discuss without restriction all religious questions that were not defined doctrine. As a consequence he was often in conflict with leaders of the Church, particularly during the late 1850s and the 1860s, when he was editor of Catholic intellectual periodicals, such as *The Rambler* (his predecessor here had been John Henry Newman) and *The Home and Foreign Review.* The provocative and sometimes arrogant manner in which he asserted his views did not help his situation.

Although Acton had been a leading (although pseudonymous)

critic of the First Vatican Council and had worked closely with his teacher, Father Johann von Dollinger, in opposing a solemn definition of papal primacy and infallibility, he refused to join him in repudiating the conciliar definitions of the papal prerogatives. Thereafter, he turned away from active involvement in religious controversy and lived undisturbed in his faith until his death in 1902, although with a deepening sense of isolation from his coreligionists.

Acton was influenced by contemporary ideas of progress and human perfectibility, and although his optimism was tempered by his dark view of human nature and his wide historical knowledge, he came to see the course of at least modern history as largely one of progress toward freedom.[1] His thought here parallels the secular optimism of many of his contemporaries, including the highly influential theories of the German evolutionary idealist G. W. F. Hegel, who believed that truth, and indeed the whole universe, progressed through a spiritual dialectic, a succession of interactions between thesis and antithesis to produce a new synthesis. Karl Marx turned this upside down with his theory of a dialectical materialism progressing inevitably to the freedom of the workers' paradise—a myth that the brutal history of the twentieth century has completely extinguished. In his historical writings Acton was always harsh on forces that opposed liberty, subjecting some popes to special condemnation and being no less severe on saints who countenanced the activities of the Inquisition. However, unlike most of late-twentieth-century Western thinkers, Acton had a liberalism rooted in Christianity, and he saw religion as fundamental both in politics and in history. As he once said, "I fully admit that political Rights proceed directly from religious duties, and hold this to be the true basis of Liberalism."[2]

---

1. John Emerich Edward Dalberg-Acton, "Inaugural Lecture on the Study of History" (1885), in *Selected Writings of Lord Acton*, vol. 2: *Essays in the Study and Writing of History*, ed. J. Rufus Fears (Indianapolis, IN: Liberty Classics, 1987), 520–21.

2. Ibid., 516.

THE BEST AND WORST OF TIMES

What would Acton say now on freedom in our Western world nearly one hundred years after his death? Certainly the terms of the debate have been changed radically since his time by the events of the twentieth century, the best of centuries and worst of centuries.

At the time of Acton's death in 1902 the British Empire appeared to be at its zenith, and European power was everywhere predominant. Today the United States is the only superpower, and unusual among superpowers because it has no external territories and because its empire is cultural and financial. Europe is still divided, while Japan, China, and India have huge economies and could well assume superpower status in the twenty-first century.

The nationalism that contributed so much to the destructive frenzy of the First World War has, at least in Europe, changed its focus in many places: for example, Wales and Scotland replacing Britain, and a collection of small nations, most recently in ex-Yugoslavia, replacing the Hapsburg Empire. Elsewhere, however, especially in the Middle East and Asia, the fires of nationalism burn fiercely, and sometimes dangerously for both internal critics and opponents and external enemies, especially when joined to Islamic fundamentalism. Regionalism and tribalism continue to present long-term threats to peace and freedom in, for example, Africa and possibly Indonesia.

The nation-states are also constrained in new ways by the international financial markets and the international business conglomerates, so that the governments of countries with small economies, for example, Australia, have little room for maneuver, especially if they prefer to live beyond their means, or close to the limit.

Acton would have applauded the Western alliance with Stalin to defeat Nazism and Japan in the Second World War and would have been firmly on the side of the Free World in the Cold War against Communism, which concluded so unexpectedly and conclusively only in the last decade of the twentieth century. He might not have been surprised by the triumph of the free market, of what Australians call "economic rationalism," although no one I know predicted its present almost universal preeminence. He would certainly have been pondering on how long this will continue, whether the seeds of decay or collapse are internal or external, and to what extent the free market system is an example of social or economic Darwinism, except that the survival of the fittest still requires the defeated, the rejects, to retain the ability to consume and purchase (or does it?). Marx's prediction of the progressive impoverishment of the workers under capitalism has proved to be completely false, as most in the Western world live in unprecedented comfort and enjoy standards of education, health, travel, and access to information never dreamed of previously.

In the Third World, almost everywhere except in parts of sub-Saharan Africa after the departure of the colonial powers, the preconditions for freedom have improved. The rise in life expectancy, the fall in infant mortality through better food and water, and improved health care have produced a huge rise in population (except in the Western world, where no country is giving birth to a sufficient number of babies to keep the population numbers constant) and better living conditions. Billions have escaped from illiteracy, and university education, at many different levels of excellence, has proliferated. India is a successful democracy (with an English-speaking middle class that provides a market for English books larger than in England itself), and democratic governments exist, sometimes precariously, throughout South America, Africa, the former Soviet Union, and many parts of Asia, as well as Europe and the English-speaking world. This represents progress and improvement.

However, the greatest intellectual puzzle for liberals in twentieth-century history is the pervasive cruelty of the Communist empires in Russia, Eastern Europe, and China. Mass cruelty is neither rare nor novel in world history, but Communism was originally idealistic. It did set out to improve the living conditions of the proletariat, industrial workers, and peasants, and tens of millions of Communists struggled and died because they saw themselves in a fight for justice. However, from its origins it was poisoned by its espousal of violence, hatred of God and religion, and systematic falsehood.

This is the other side to the twentieth century, and its nature and its significance for nineteenth-century liberal intellectuals like Acton is well captured in these lines from Solzhenitsyn's *The Gulag Archipelago:*

If the intellectuals in the plays of Chekhov who spent all their time guessing what would happen in twenty, or thirty or forty years time had been told that in forty years interrogation by torture would be [routinely] practiced in Russia; that prisoners would have their skulls squeezed within iron rings; that a human being would be lowered into an acid bath; that they would be trussed up naked to be bitten by ants and bedbugs; that a ramrod heated over a primus stove would be thrust up their anal canal ('the secret brand'); that a man's genitals would be slowly crushed beneath the toe of a jackboot; and that, in the luckiest possible circumstances, prisoners would be tortured by being kept from sleeping for a week, by thirst, and by being beaten to a bloody pulp, not one of Chekhov's plays would have gotten to its end because all the heroes would have gone off to an insane asylum.[3]

By the most conservative estimates, at least 85 to 100 million people have been killed this century by Communist governments.[4] The largest number of deaths occurred in Russia and China, "to the point where the million or so executed by the Khmer Rouge are well within the margin of error for the total."[5]

The Nazis also killed millions through internal oppression, as well as the 40 to 50 million dead (military and civilian) in the Second World War, which they (with Japan) unleashed—the deadliest war in history. The best known example of this Nazi infamy is the

3. Aleksandr Solzhenitsyn, *The Gulag Archipelago*, abridged ed., ed. Edward E. Ericson Jr., trans. Thomas P. Whitney and Harry Willetts (London: Collins Harvill, 1986), 39.
4. Stéphane Courtois et al., *The Black Book of Communism.*
5. Gary Saul Morson, "How Did Dostoyevsky Know?" *New Criterion* 17:9 (May 1999): 21–30, at 21.

Holocaust, the systematic extermination of Jews simply because they were Jews. In most Western eyes this crime against humanity is the crime of the century.

This is certainly appropriate, but I regret the silence and negligence that surround Communist crimes. Nearly all the twelve-year-olds I speak to know of Hitler; very few have heard of Stalin. I could not even obtain a tax deduction for donations to the descendants of the prisoners of the Gulag, who survive today, millions of them, in Siberia, originally from many different nations.

The immense killing power of the totalitarian state in this century has been increased by the superior technology of our age. But this is not the whole story. Eight and a half million died in battle in the First World War, but Stalin killed 14.5 million in his war against the peasantry through the primitive means of starvation, beatings, and exposure.[6] The same applies to most of Pol Pot's one to two million victims. Even the Nazis, who industrialized human extermination at Auschwitz and other places, managed to kill hundreds of thousands of Jews in Russia by the simple means of burying them alive. None of this required high-tech. What it did require was a certain sort of "social technology"[7]—a combination of bureaucracy, rationalization, ideology, and total power; a lethal combination of lying propaganda spread by modern communications, evil leaders, and compliant followers as well as technology.

So much of this death and destruction has been caused by, or in the fight against, the savage anti-God parties of Lenin, Stalin, Hitler, Mao, and Pol Pot. The struggle against these ideologies has been a struggle against lies: lies about human nature, about the worth of the human individual and certain ethnic or social groups, and not least about man's freedom. One of the great lessons of the twentieth century concerns the conditions under which human

6. Robert Conquest, *Harvest of Sorrow: Soviet Collectivization and the Terror-Famine* (New York: Oxford University Press, 1986), chapter 16.
7. Morson, "How Did Dostoyevsky Know?" 25.

freedom and human dignity can flourish, and they do not flourish under regimes based on lies.

At this stage one might be tempted to remark that we have wandered far from Acton's world, and indeed far from local Australian concerns. However, Australians fought in both World Wars, as well as the anti-Communist wars in Korea, Malaysia, and Vietnam. The Communists were never an electoral threat here, but were powerful in many unions during and after the Second World War.

Given our geography, we must be interested in Asia, and even in this age of jet travel and instant communications we remain very far away from our rich and powerful English-speaking friends who protected us, and indeed saved us, in the twentieth century. Australians are great travelers; we realize we must know the wider world and be involved with it, not least to learn what might befall us if we betray our heritage of law, democracy, and freedom. Most people are tempted to condone some level of totalitarianism in what they judge to be a good cause; we are and will continue to be susceptible to these temptations, like everyone else.

More to the point is the need to identify the forces in Western culture that will help us make sense of our changing world, especially as they touch on the themes of freedom and Christianity, the predominant religion of the West and in Australia, where 64 percent of the population still calls themselves Christian.

MODERN MAN AND FREEDOM

One guide is the French philosopher Pierre Manent, who teaches at the *École des Hautes Études en Sciences Sociales* in Paris. A convert to Catholicism, he trained under the great French sociologist Raymond Aron and locates himself expressly in the tradition of Alexis de Tocqueville.

For Tocqueville the democratic revolution of the late eighteenth and nineteenth century brought modern man into existence. In describing the nature of the democratic revolution and what it portends for the future, Tocqueville was at once troubled and absorbed by the particular human type or ideal that it called into being, although he tells us very little about its origins. This provides Manent with his point of departure, and in *The City of Man* (1994) he traces the intellectual developments in European history that were to make modern man possible. The title itself is a poignant contrast with the early-fifth-century work of St. Augustine, *The City of God*, which this North African bishop wrote to allay the fears of his fellow Christians after the city of Rome had been sacked by the barbarian Goths, the first such desecration for eight hundred years.

Manent is quite clear that the concept of modern man is no mere self-flattering conceit. Our historical predecessors can appear to us as an entirely different sort of animal, and we can feel ourselves to be separated from them by an enormous gulf. This is compounded by the willful manner in which history is often misrepresented, as a means of both encouraging a sense of superiority over the past and denying its hold on us as either authority or tradition.

This is particularly so, in Manent's view, when it comes to understanding the origins and meaning of Western culture and the dynamic at work within it. The West is the product of a dialogue between what Manent calls "the party of nature"—that is, the classical inheritance of the Greco-Roman world—and "the party of grace"—by which he means the revelation of the Christian religion. The party of nature emphasizes pride, magnanimity, and the cultivation of the virtues that are natural to man. The party of grace emphasizes humility, renunciation, and the cultivation of the soul.[8] The dialogue between them is "fraught with conflict," and the tension this generates gives Western culture its peculiar dynamism.[9] But the dialogue was made possible only by an underlying

8. Russell Hittinger, "What Is Man?" *First Things* 88 (December 1998): 42–44, at 42.

9. Pierre Manent, *The City of Man* (1994), trans. Marc A. LePain (Princeton, NJ: Princeton University Press, 1998), 24–25.

solidarity between the two parties, something that Thomas Aquinas made explicit in his great philosophical synthesis of classical and Christian thought in the thirteenth century.[10]

However, the dialogue took a different course especially in the eighteenth century. Over time, the parties "turned on one another like two grindstones"[11] and sought to deny each other's legitimacy. Modernity was born when the relationship between the two parties became "cultural war," where victory is impossible and the two sides are pitted against each other to forge a new humanity: revelation's demand for holiness and renunciation against the self-assertion of the party of the nature, and the grace of freedom against the demands and restrictions of nature.[12]

In this way modern man emerged, who understands himself as someone above and beyond both nature and transcendence, and who rejects both those traditional authorities. Emphasizing freedom against nature and animality against transcendence, he celebrates the fact that he, not any source of authority, creates his own values, and the concept of holiness is ignored as superfluous.[13] All this is reflected in the world modern man makes, a world dominated by technology and utility, where people are urged to become radical individualists who are their own supreme measure of things and incorrigible consumers, for whom comfort and good health are absolutes.

Manent's style of analysis is not Australian, nor even typical of the English-speaking world, but it is illuminating even for Australia, where the two grindstones of the Greco-Roman inheritance and an articulate public expression of Judeo-Christianity have never been at war in quite the same way as the French have been intermittently since at least 1789. Both these traditions retain considerable influence in our parliaments and law courts and perhaps in some business circles; less among academics and the media, where a variegated secularism flourishes.

10. Ibid., 33–34.   11. Ibid., 27.
12. Hittinger, "What Is Man?" 43.   13. Ibid.

CATHOLICS AND THE DONALD DUCK HERESY

What contribution might the Catholic intellectual tradition make to the debate on freedom and the closely related question of human rights? How might the Catholic communities throughout the world work to maintain or develop and change the notion of freedom? Is the Christian concept of freedom much different from the freedom admired by Westerners, if there is any such single concept? After all, Christians have been talking about freedom since the first New Testament writings of St Paul, who was certainly very bossy with the communities he led.

The Oxford historian of ideas Isaiah Berlin in his celebrated 1958 lecture on "Two Concepts of Liberty" followed Acton in mentioning that two hundred different meanings of the word *freedom* have been recorded,[14] although he introduced the terminology of negative freedom (freedom to be or to act without external interference) and positive freedom (the ambition of most people to be their own master, to be self-directed, a subject with a capacity to do this rather than that). He also remarks that these two concepts of freedom can come into conflict.[15] In the English-speaking world most people would interpret liberty in the classical English sense, following John Stuart Mill (unknowingly), as doing our own good in our own way, without hurting others, and without too much government interference, much less imprisonment or other forms of violence. We each want a fair go.

Once we try to implement these commonplace notions we are confronted with an interesting series of dilemmas. Should a person be free not to wear a seat belt in a car? Should a woman be free to have an abortion? Does the father of the child have any rights here? Does the embryo, fetus, human being, or unborn child (however defined) have any rights? Should persons be free to perform "mercy killings" (euthanasia)?

14. Isaiah Berlin, *The Proper Study of Mankind*, ed. Henry Hardy (New York: Farrar, Straus and Giroux, 1998), 193.
15. Ibid., 194, 204.

These dilemmas also touch governments and business. To what extent should governments be morally neutral or indifferent, leaving the strong to triumph and the poor to go to the wall? Or should governments work for the common good? To what extent should businesses be free to maximize profits, or do they have obligations to build up the positive freedom of their workers and customers through just family wages, reasonable hours, and accessible prices? Are business answers found entirely in economic imperatives and Adam Smith's "invisible hand," or are there ethical limits? Is business constrained by virtue as well as economic necessity?

The old centrally controlled Communist governments used the economy and every other aspect of state apparatus ostensibly to work for equality. This was never achieved, although the living standards of hundreds of millions were raised, but at a terrible cost to freedom. With this Communist collapse we now see more clearly that it is impossible to reconcile freedom with egalitarianism and even equality in most situations. Even with children, do we work for equality of opportunity or equality of outcomes? Or does a truly free society, or human nature itself, require that there cannot even be equality of opportunity?

These are hard questions, and the writings of the Polish philosopher-pope John Paul II help throw light on them. John Paul II had the unusual advantage of having lived under the Nazis, under the Communists, and in the free world. He experienced these different systems as a lay university student and conscript to forced labor, then as a seminarian, priest, and bishop. He went into the conclave that elected him pope reading a Marxist intellectual journal.[16]

John Paul II was the first pope to give a thorough critique of culture. He was popularly portrayed as being driven primarily by an interest in specific and tough moral norms against abortion, contraception, homosexuality, and euthanasia, despite his powerful encyclicals on public life and the economy. But the truth is

16. Weigel, *Witness to Hope*, 252.

that from his early days as a young philosophy teacher one of his central preoccupations was the topic of freedom and responsibility. The major ethical contribution he made during his pontificate, and preceding it, was in fact a critique of Western culture's view of freedom and a demonstration of freedom's connection with truth, particularly the truths expressed in the natural moral law.

John Paul II believed that one section of affluent Western thought (Manent's modern man) has radically misconceived freedom. Freedom is generally understood here by the model of a smorgasbord of options: the more options we have, the greater our freedom. No matter if the options on the table include fatty foods, foods low in nutrition, foods full of sugar and preservatives or even poisons: freedom is simply having the widest possible range of options and making one's *own* choice, whether this is actually good for oneself and others or not. Any attempt to influence choice-making—law, duties, rights, religion—is seen as an unfortunate restraint, to be resisted.

John Paul II's view was that there is no true conflict between freedom of choice and moral law. All Christians believe that each human person has a rational intellect and a free will. We are free, in different measures, to build slowly an integrated personality, without gross contradictions. But this is a life-long spiritual quest. God-given law is not some legalistic imposition but consists rather of truths meant to help human persons make good moral choices and in this way truly to fulfill themselves. In this alone will they achieve the dignity of persons who pursue their true end freed from subservience to arbitrary feelings and obsessions in a free choice of the good.

Ultimately, then, the view of positive freedom we should take is not one of increasing options and reducing guidance concerning them, but one of encouraging intelligent deliberation about which options best accord with real human fulfillment. Unlimited negative freedom, the absence of external restraints, would produce chaos in our society as surely as it would on our roads. A key need for thinking about freedom today is to explore further this notion of genuine human fulfillment in the face of the many crude versions of subjectivism and relativism sweeping our society.

One practical conclusion from this is that Catholics should stop talking about the primacy of conscience. This has never been a Catholic doctrine (although this point generally cuts little ice), and such language is not conducive to identifying what contributes to human development. It is a shortcut, which often leads the uninitiated to feel even more complacent while "doing their own thing."

Sometimes primacy-of-conscience advocates also insist that the Church apologize for the crimes against freedom committed by Christians, for example, in the Crusades, in the Inquisition, or against the indigenous peoples. But against what standard might these deeds be judged? Who is to say that our conscience is superior to the consciences of those living in earlier times? It is only when we concede that our consciences stand under the principles of truth and justice, or perhaps under the Word of God revealed in the Scriptures, that we can begin to consider the prudence of apologies for particular crimes.

Another way of explaining the task of all in the Judeo-Christian tradition is to insist that we must resist what the English historian Felipe Fernández-Armesto calls "the Lone Ranger heresy" and "the Donald Duck heresy."[17]

In the Lone Ranger syndrome the hero is always an outsider who spurns society, who will not acknowledge that genuine individuality always needs reciprocity. Even well-intentioned Lone Rangers are dangerous and alienating.

Of greater import for our purposes is the Donald Duck heresy, which rests squarely on the fallacy of overwhelming natural virtue. All you have to do to fulfill yourself is follow your natural impulses. Donald Duck always does this and always gets into trouble. It is a heresy that sanctifies mistakes, provided one is genuine, being oneself.

17. Felipe Fernández-Armesto, "America Can Still Save the World," *Spectator*, 8 January 2000.

Donald Duck is amusing, even lovable up to a point, and this intriguing but trivial example should not distract us from the dangers already around us, especially visible in the United States. We need to pause, because what happens in North America today recurs on many occasions in Australia at a later date.

The celebration of Woodstock's thirtieth anniversary in 1999, held in New York state at an old B52 bomber base inappropriately called Rome, was particularly disturbing. Unfortunately all the rioting, arson, looting of $170,000 from a mobile bank, drug taking, and gang rapes at this event did not represent an untypical lapse, were not just examples of the passing foolishness of youth, but were an inevitable progression from the first love fest, as surely an indication of social disintegration as the Columbine High School massacre.

Thirty years of myth making should not conceal the darker side of the first Woodstock, celebrating peace and love. As one participant said, there was a shortage of toilets, mud, delays, and drug overdoses everywhere as well as the inevitable measure of sexual exploitation; but it was peaceful. The participants of both gatherings rejected their parents' values. But this time it was the pacifism of the sixties that was spurned, as more than a dozen bonfires of trucks and tents blazed and mobs used iron bars to smash and trash. A violent minority, no doubt influenced by an ugly mixture of drink and drugs, were heavily into fighting as well as fornication. Either the restraints of thirty years ago were no longer effective or the self-hatred, anger, and alienation of the destructive minority were stronger and were incited rather than restrained by the music. The last song of the gathering, as the ambulance sirens wailed through the smoke and the mayhem, boomed out from a group called Cracker. Its chorus summed up the scene: "Don't f— me up with peace and love."[18]

It would be unfair to the United States and too bleak and pes-

18. Roger Franklin, "The Spirit of Woodstock on the Eve of Destruction," *Sunday Age*, 1 August 1999.

simistic to conclude at this point. The violent were only a small part the of the three hundred thousand at Woodstock '99, and Woodstock in turn is only a small part of the U.S.A. And very definitely, Australia is different from North America.

In Australia we have a long tradition of stable government and stable communities. We are part of that proud minority of nations whose birth was not accompanied or followed by war or violence. We cherish our freedom and take the protection of these freedoms seriously. We value the separation of powers, the benign separation of church and state, and practice the politics of persuasion. Political parties regularly move from government into opposition, and vice versa; and all sections of society, including the religious groupings, understand that in a democracy you have to be prepared to have the majority decide against you. In other words there is at present no discernible and significant threat to our traditional freedoms. Neither George Orwell's *1984* nor Aldous Huxley's *Brave New World* is on the horizon.

This is not a claim to Australian innocence, not a denial of our mistakes and crimes with the aborigines, of the sad number of abortions each year, of the high level of youth unemployment. Nor does it deny the possibility of a new permanent underclass emerging, battered by family breakdown, unemployment, alcohol, drugs, gambling, and sexual irresponsibility. In fact the greater danger to freedom is likely to come from the evil consequences of spreading social disintegration, rather than from the exponents of political correctness imposing their precepts on us all. But it is a claim that we have a culture of freedom that we cherish, and a tradition of robust, sometimes confrontational, dialogue that rests confidently on social solidarity.

Nor does any major religious group in Australia make claims to innocence, least of all the Catholic Church. But the Christian contribution to shaping Australian consciousness has been profound.

There is an "architecture of freedom," which is a human construct, not a natural ecology, built on that longing for freedom which is one of the hallmarks of our time.[19] Perhaps the Catholic task is not only to teach and explain that life is good and meaningful, but that as peace is the fruit of justice, so true freedom requires truth and is the fruit of consistently striving for what is good. The public benefits and consequences of Christian living need to be spelled out and defended at the ballot box. The dialogue with tradition should continue within our contemporary pluralism, while we work relentlessly to show that the Woodstock conception of liberty only traps people into "the jungle chaos of their hidden emotions," damaging and sometimes destroying them and their victims.

The Christian tradition reveres the martyrs, those who sacrifice their freedom and indeed their life for a higher cause. Despite their misfortune we claim that in their soul, their heart of hearts, they retain not only their integrity, but their personal freedom to choose. For all people of integrity the Truth has set them free.[20]

19. John Paul II, "Address to the 50th General Assembly of the United Nations," New York, 5 October 1995, §12.
20. Cf. Jn. 8:31–32.

4. CATHOLICISM AND DEMOCRACY

Describing Australia as a secular society has become almost a throw-away line, but the reality is different. Data from the 2001 Census showed that 68 percent (64 percent in 2006) of Australians describe themselves as Christian, and about 75 percent believe in God.[1] The Australian Community Survey indicates that two-thirds of Australians believe a spiritual life is important to them, and 70 percent have some contact with the Christian churches each year. Thirty-three percent of the population say they pray or meditate at least weekly.[2]

None of this evidence is consistent with the claim that Australia is basically a secular country. Rather this claim reflects the fact that among academics, journalists, and other members of the commentariat the religious situation is roughly the obverse of what it is in the general community. People in these privileged positions mainly mix with people like themselves, and this can cause spectacular errors of judgment. The American historian and social commentator Gertrude Himmelfarb once told of an academic who was convinced that a conspiracy had made Ronald Reagan president of the United States, because no one he knew had voted for him.[3] This is like our situation, where a disproportionately secular opinion-forming class assumes that everyone else is secular too.

Many of Australia's important secular institutions owe their

This chapter was originally presented as "The Catholic Contribution to a Christian Australia," Jubilee Lecture, Catholic Institute of Sydney, 26 May 2004.

1. Philip Hughes, "Trends in Religious Identification: Details from the 2001 Census," *Pointers: Bulletin of the Christian Research Association* 12:3 (September 2002): 1–4.

2. Ibid.

3. Gertrude Himmelfarb, "Democratic Remedies for Democratic Disorders," *Public Interest* 131 (Spring 1998): 3–24.

origins to Christianity. The university is a medieval Christian invention, and enjoyed considerable autonomy from secular and ecclesiastical authority from its foundation—not just from the time
of the Renaissance as the traditional mythology would have it.
The American sociologist Rodney Stark has argued that an institution such as the university was possible only in a culture founded
on belief in a conscious, rational, and all-powerful Creator. Western science had its origins in the same theology, and the advantage
the West had over other cultures was precisely its conviction that
God was reasonable and that his work in creation was also reasonable, predictable, and intelligible to us.[4] The belief in the basic in-
telligibility of the world, although under attack from philosophical claims that insist that there is no such thing as truth, is still a
foundational assumption of the so-called secular societies of the
West such as Australia.

Hospitals and schools are more basic examples of institutions
that we take for granted that also had their beginnings in Christian convents and monasteries. Even secular democracy is workable
only on the basis of Christian assumptions about human dignity,
respect for persons, natural rights, the common good, and tolerance and compassion.[5] These principles do not come about simply
by bringing people together in a community. It is frequently observed today in relation to events in the Arab world that democracy is not something that can be imposed; that democracy needs a
certain sort of culture to make it possible. For the West, that culture is fundamentally Christian.

The secularism of modern democracy continues to rely on
the cultural capital bequeathed it by Christianity. While I rejoice in
the separation of church and state, it is inaccurate to claim Australian society is secular. This raises the question of the sustainability
of our most important institutions in the long term as the Christian cultural capital on which they depend is eaten up and not re-

4. Stark, *For the Glory of God*, chapter 2.
5. Rodney Stark, *The Victory of Reason* (New York: Random House, 2005), chapter 3.

newed. One area where this is already assuming critical importance is in the law, particularly as it deals with rights and the conflict of rights. The link between rights and natural law has long been sundered, and it is not clear that either democracy or the idea of rights has been well served by this development. The Church has an important contribution to make here, but perhaps before outlining this it would help to set out a few general observations on the contribution that faith makes to culture in the modern situation.

THE CONTRIBUTION OF RELIGION TO DEMOCRATIC CULTURE

The particular contribution that the Church has made to Australia differs from that made in other places. There is no surprise in this. We are used to comparisons of our own situation with that in the United States, and this seems a good rule to follow here, not least because of the powerful impact that American culture and developments have throughout the world.

While evangelical Anglicanism in places like Sydney is strong and evangelical communities are growing, this is yet to translate in Australia into a clear public voice of the sort commanded by groups such as the Southern Baptists and the Christian Coalition in America. For the moment this absence is one significant difference between Australia and the United States in matters of religion. In Australia the movement of these groups toward more active participation in public affairs has not always been welcomed. In 2001, when the Anglican Archbishop of Sydney, Dr. Peter Jensen, suggested that Christians should do more to evangelize Australian society, the *Sydney Morning Herald* published an editorial condemning this idea as arrogant and dangerous, and a recipe for bloodshed. Observing that "in Australia, one's religion is largely a private matter," the editorial concluded—with only a small hint of menace—that "it should remain that way."[6] This editorial epito-

6. Editorial, "Freedom of Belief," *Sydney Morning Herald*, 21 August 2001.

mized a certain secular attitude to traditional religion that tolerates some of it for the sake of "diversity" but only on the condition that it is privatized.[7]

This is not a deal that Australian Catholic Church leaders have generally been willing to accept. The Catholic Church in Australia has been blessed with bishops, such as Cardinal Patrick Francis Moran in Sydney (1884–1911) and Archbishop Daniel Mannix in Melbourne (1917–63), who were prepared on occasion to be a little outspoken. Moran opposed anti-Chinese legislation in the 1880s and 1890s, denounced French anti-Semitism during the Dreyfus affair, and was a vocal supporter of female suffrage, trade unionism, the new Labor Party and the governments it formed in New South Wales, and an independent defense and foreign policy for Australia. His involvement in the political affairs of the day even went to the extent of his standing (unsuccessfully) for election in 1897 to the Australasian Federal Convention, which wrote the Australian constitution. Mannix played a critical part in the successful campaign to oppose conscription in World War I, was a tireless defender of Catholic schools, immigrants, and unions, and had a genius for encouraging lay people to take part in political life, one of the most important examples of which was his support of Bob Santamaria's efforts to counter Communist infiltration of the union movement. Australia's much smaller population made it easier for bishops such as Moran and Mannix to secure nationwide influence, an advantage their brother bishops in America may not have enjoyed to the same extent. In Australia this has been good for the Church and good for democracy.

The privatization of belief is usually justified by referring to the importance of maintaining the public domain and public policy as "neutral" areas. But privatization does not favor neutrality. It is a way of silencing opponents and as such favors the dominant secular cultural identity. The privatization of belief was basically

7. M. A. Casey, "The Politics of Meaninglessness," *Sydney Papers* 15:3–4 (Winter–Spring 2003): 136–43, at 142.

the solution that John F. Kennedy proposed to reassure American voters that it was safe to put a Catholic in the White House.[8] As an old Kennedy groupie I say this with some sadness. One effect, in the United States at least, has been to raise up a generation of Catholic legislators who seem to think it is possible to be openly pro-abortion in their work and still be a Catholic in good standing.

The Catholic Church was slow to give public approval to democracy. The main reason for this is that the nineteenth century, which we now see from our perspective as the period when democracy inexorably began to replace other forms of government in the West, offered to contemporaries many examples of experiments in democracy going wrong, beginning of course with the French Revolution. Many of these governments were also hostile to Catholicism.[9] For this reason the Church's teaching in philosophy and theology about democracy is still young, although indi-

8. On 12 September 1960 Kennedy told a group of Southern Baptist leaders in Houston:

I believe in an America where the separation of church and state is absolute— where no Catholic prelate would tell the President (should he be a Catholic) how to act and no Protestant minister would tell his parishioners for whom to vote—where no church or church school is granted any public funds or political preference—and where no man is denied public office merely because his religion differs from the President who might appoint him or the people who might elect him.

Later on in his talk, by way of spelling out what this meant for him as a Catholic, Kennedy emphasized that

I am not the Catholic candidate for President [but the candidate] who happens also to be a Catholic. I do not speak for my church on public matters— and the church does not speak for me.

Whatever issue may come before me as President, if I should be elected—on birth control, divorce, censorship, gambling, or any other subject—I will make my decision in accordance with these views, in accordance with what my conscience tells me to be in the national interest, and without regard to outside religious pressure or dictate. And no power or threat of punishment could cause me to decide otherwise.

For the full text of this speech, see *New York Times*, 13 September 1960.

9. George Pell, "*Rerum novarum* One Hundred Years Later" (Boston University: The Boston Conversazione, 1992).

vidual Catholic thinkers have made important contributions outside the magisterium.[10]

One famously important thinker about democracy (and the French Revolution) is Alexis de Tocqueville (1805–59). Tocqueville believed that the premises of secularism do not sustain democracy but undermine it, encouraging a lowering of personal taste and public standards, as well as materialism and moral relativism.[11] The end of this would be, he claimed, a new soft despotism, imprisonment by a thousand silken threads.[12] Against this danger, the faith of the West offers a belief in the inherent dignity of each person, made in God's likeness; a belief in the equality of all humans in God's sight, whatever their natural inequalities; and a belief in the centrality of liberty in the purposes of the one true God for the cosmos.[13]

In a democracy, religion should strengthen and correct morals and manners, not so much by its contributions to lawmaking (although this too is important), as by its influence on daily living and especially in the family and the home, where stable morals and good order remain the basis of civilized life.[14] Moral clarity is a great gain, especially in times of crisis, and the Christian concepts of God and especially human nature are indispensable helps to daily living. Faith also goes beyond a morality of mere reason by introducing the notion of immortality, life after death, whose quality will be decided by a personal and undeceivable Judge.[15]

Tocqueville wrote that the apparently opposed "spirits" of

10. Examples of Catholic thinkers who either directly or indirectly addressed the question of democracy positively, and prior to the Second Vatican Council, include Frédéric Ozanam, G. K. Chesterton, Jacques Maritain, Christopher Dawson, and Fr. John Courtney Murray, S.J.

11. Alexis de Tocqueville, *Democracy in America* (1835 & 1840), ed. and trans. Harvey C. Mansfield and Delba Winthrop (Chicago: University of Chicago Press, 2000), 417–24.

12. Ibid., 661–65.

13. Stark, *The Victory of Reason*.

14. Tocqueville, *Democracy in America*, 558–63.

15. Cf. Mt. 25: 31–46.

religion and freedom do not harm one another but "advance in accord and seem to lend each other a mutual support." "Religion sees in civil freedom a noble exercise of the faculties of man," and "freedom sees in religion the companion of its struggles and triumphs, the cradle of its infancy, and the divine source of its rights," and also the guarantee of its own duration.[16] In Tocqueville's assessment, religion should be considered as the first of democracy's institutions. "Despotism can do without faith, but freedom cannot."[17]

The blessings we enjoy in Western societies are in no small part due to the way Christianity has informed and guided our most important institutions. But this will not remain the case automatically. Wisdom and hard work are needed to defend democracy and the culture of freedom within which it exists, both from its critics and also from its friends. Carelessly, or purposefully, claiming that secularism is equivalent to neutrality, or that secularism provides the only level playing field, can and does lead to developments such as those in Canada and Australia, where anti-discrimination commissions have been used in an attempt to silence Christians who criticize same-sex marriage or Islam.[18] This is not good for religion, and it is certainly not good for democracy.

THE CASE AGAINST RIGHTS

For several decades, the Catholic Church has explained moral truths and their application to social issues using the concept and rhetoric of rights. Reasons for this include the attempt to use the secular grammar of rights as a basis for a dialogue with secular-

---

16. Tocqueville, *Democracy in America*, 43–44.

17. Ibid., 280–82.

18. On the situation in Canada, see Raymond J. de Souza, "Thinly Disguised Totalitarianism," *First Things* 142 (April 2004): 9–12. On the prosecution of two Christian pastors under anti-vilification laws in Victoria, Australia, for criticizing Islam, see Daveed Gartenstein-Ross, "Legislating Religious Correctness," *Weekly Standard*, 27 October 2005.

ists and the strong belief by some Catholics that "rights-talk" is a good vehicle for advancing a Catholic understanding of justice, morality, and the common good. But one of the downsides for the Church and Catholic thinkers is that it exposes us to the danger of either embracing democracy uncritically and seeking to make our peace with it at any price or, at the other extreme, resuming a hostile or defensive position toward democratic politics.

Some in the Church argue that Catholics should not use what Alasdair MacIntyre has called this "dubious idiom and rhetoric of rights."[19] Among these are Australian theologian Tracey Rowland, who has made a first-rate attempt to look critically at the Church's engagement with modernity, and our relations with contemporary culture generally, in her book *Culture and the Thomist Tradition after Vatican II* (2003). The book is rich and substantial, and a call to serious discussion about the language and assumptions of contemporary moral and social debate.

Philosophically Rowland echoes the view of MacIntyre that moral terms belong to a particular tradition and narrative, and that, for example, taking rights-talk from post-Enlightenment secularism and attempting to use it to further the claims of classical Thomism is incoherent.[20] MacIntyre argues that liberals and Thomists will mean radically different things by "rights," and the lack of a shared conception of the common good means that the appearance of agreement is a façade concealing serious dangers for Christianity.[21]

Rowland believes that using secular language to set out Catholic claims makes it easier for Catholics to slip into a secular understanding of autonomy and freedom, hostile especially to the hard teachings of the Gospel. We need to recognize, she argues, that Catholic language and symbols are part-constitutive of the tradi-

---

19. Alasdair MacIntyre, "Community, Law, and the Idiom and Rhetoric of Rights," *Listening* 24:2 (1991): 96–110, at 96–97.

20. Tracey Rowland, *Culture and the Thomist Tradition after Vatican II* (London: Routledge, 2003), chapter 7.

21. MacIntyre, "Community, Law, and the Idiom and Rhetoric of Rights," 108.

tion and that moving from these is theologically dangerous.[22] It is accepting the appearance of short-term agreement in place of the deep and difficult debate that believers need to have with secular liberalism.

Rowland opens up much that is important in the debate, but we should not exaggerate the dangers of speaking to contemporary society. The Church's clear preference for modern democracy and its commitment to human rights as a proper goal of democracy coexist well with a traditional Catholic approach to faith and morals—they certainly do so in the teaching of Pope John Paul II. It is relatively early days yet for the Catholic option for democracy and rights. Our teaching on rights is coherent with our anthropology, with the natural law tradition of Aquinas, and with the moral principles with which we approach bioethical, sexual, and other human issues, such as social justice. We are all aware of the enormous secular pressure on church leaders and Christian politicians to mind their own spiritual and religious business, and to leave the question of which values the community should adopt to those who can consider it in an "unbiased"—that is, secular—fashion. This is not a position that Christians can ever accept. The Church's intervention in the public domain is crucial—in particular, its interventions on behalf of those unable to speak for themselves—and one of the important grounds on which Church leaders base their interventions is fundamental human rights. Abandoning rights is not an option for the twenty-first-century Church.

Thinkers such as Rowland, MacIntyre, and David Schindler who counsel about the dangers of any sell-out to secular liberalism do an important service.[23] But there is need for moderation. The Catholic Church is a great church and not a sect. The critical question is the nature of the terms in our dialogue with modernity. The Enlightenment and post-Enlightenment worlds are not

22. Rowland, *Culture and the Thomist Tradition*, 151–52.

23. See, for example, David L. Schindler, *Heart of the World, Center of the Church* (Edinburgh: T. and T. Clark, 1996).

such strangers to our own tradition that we have nothing to say to them and everything to fear. The Enlightenment itself is in many ways a child of Christianity, however unexpected and puzzling the offspring. Indeed, Enlightenment modernity fails to understand itself fully unless it acknowledges its Christian roots and context: how can we understand Hume without the background of Calvinist faith and ethics to which he is responding? The French Enlightenment thinkers without Jansenism? The existentialists and deconstructionists of our own times without the traditions of Christian essentialism and Christian authority against which they are rebelling? We may feel we have little in common with these other traditions, but as in all families with messy genealogies, there is still enough common DNA around for us to speak (parts of) each other's language, while being wary of the dangers of compromise.

THE CLASH OF RIGHTS

Rights matter, but rights-talk does not exhaust the meaning of faith. In particular, Christian faith looks askance at those who would interpret the whole of life in terms of our own personal claims. People of faith are at least as concerned for the rights of others as for their own rights, and are more concerned about the rights of those in serious need than about their own rights. They are also concerned about duties, and not just the duties of the state or the church or other unnamed agencies, but our personal obligation to move beyond our comfort zone and to work at personal cost to satisfy the needs of others.

We believe in this demanding approach to rights because we believe it reflects moral truth. Thus part of my answer to Rowland, and others, is that Christian rights-talk is not simply claims based on wishes—like the rights-talk of the secular liberal—but claims in justice based on moral truths about the person. The claims of all persons in each different society to obtain at least the minimum requirements, usually through work, in order to flourish is a moral truth; and so far as the rights of the person are based on such a perception of moral truth they are very real and very serious. As John Finnis argues, "if its logic and its place in a reasonable approach to human flourishing are kept in mind, the modern usage of 'right' as the principal counter in political discourse should be recognized . . . as a valuable addition."[24]

This raises the important issue of the denial of rights to some individuals and minorities, and the vital role of the Church in speaking up for victims at such times. If rights are claims to just treatment concerning important human goods, then children's rights will be at the head of our moral wish lists today. Children, like all of us, have a right to life, to health care, to truth, and to a family. But in their case these rights are even more important, given their youth and vulnerability. Naturally, not everyone can always be given all to which they have a right: death, or other lesser tragedies, makes orphans of children. Yet the natural right to be loved and reared by mother and father is a matter of justice that ought to be supported by moral custom, wider society, and legislation. For individuals to deny their obligations to their children is appalling. For the state to deny the common obligation to children by encouraging the breakdown of marriage and family should appall us even more.

Our human rights tradition requires us to protect (if only by moral argumentation) the proper rights of children when they are disregarded by a minority of adults who are demanding satisfaction of their aberrant personal choices—for example, to leave spouse and children. Supporting marriage and family is just one way in which strong religious belief and belief in human rights combined can help expose the pseudo-rights of modernity. Modern rights are very often not human rights. They are not claims based on the truth about the human good and common good. Rather, they are products of convention or fashion, based on no more than an exaggerated claim for autonomy and the chosen life-style-values of minorities. The claims of "thin" rights like these should always be trumped by the human rights claims defended in Catholic teaching and supported by natural law thinking.

A commitment to human rights will also mean an interest in policy questions. Of course the Church claims no expertise in economics or the social sciences and has no mandate for partisan interventions in political debate. Yet a policy that, for example, reduced the minimum wage beneath what a parent needs to maintain a family, offered tax breaks to high-earning singles, or smoothed and widened the path to divorce or abortion or access to artificial reproductive technologies would be a policy that raised major human rights questions, questions in which the Catholic Church has an interest because of her God-given mandate to care for persons, families, and all in serious need.

The age of terror in which we now live has followed a brief decade of unchallenged secular liberalism, a decade that, in turn, followed the eventual collapse of the Communist nightmare in 1989. We do not know how events will now unfold, but it seems that for many, Christian voices will be important, prophetic, necessary. The issues at stake today are large, and secular liberalism now looks rather smaller, rather more confused, less able to deal with the new, vast political realities.

In the new situation religion will play a key role, and the witness of Christians for those in need—for love and not for violence, for service and not for triumph—will continue to be important. But dogmatic liberalism still attempts to silence the Church's contribution. Liberalism ought in principle to give everyone a voice, and an equal voice. That is what liberalism means. But in fact dogmatic secular liberals increasingly use liberalism to exclude the voice of the Church.

Throughout the West calls are regularly heard for the Church to stay out of public debates on medical and bioethical issues. The liberal rhetoric may say "all have an equal voice at the table," but the dogmatic secularist holds "only our liberal friends are really free to speak."[25] Such dogmatism may be of little help in the age of terror. The Catholic Church, however, has a moral wisdom and expertise to offer, based on the ethics of love for our enemies and of justice for all. The challenge from liberalism will continue, but we can ponder that liberalism now has less to boast about and rather less to say since September 11.

FAITH AND DEMOCRACY

Meanwhile, we must continue to exist and to flourish within a pluralist liberal democracy. How do we respond to those who argue for new and anti-Christian approaches to family, to the status of the embryo, to those who are terminally ill or unconscious? If people do not share our faith, how do we respond to the accusation that we are simply imposing Christian values on a secular state? We can of course state that our central moral arguments are based not only on revealed truth but on natural law truths, accessible to all people of good will and clear mind. But from a society such as ours that rejects such a moral theory, accepting instead an ethic of preference-satisfaction and pragmatism, large-scale agreement cannot be expected.

Another response might begin with a discussion on the real nature of participatory democracy and the Church's role in democratic debate. In *Evangelium vitae* John Paul II addressed the moral legitimacy of a democracy. There is no more a divine right for a democracy to do as it wishes than there was a divine right of kings to do so. Democracy is not to be "idolized," treated as an infallible voice of wisdom, an adjudication always to be followed and never to be questioned.[26] It is useful to remember Winston Churchill's verdict in 1947 in the House of Commons: "No one pretends that

25. This is certainly the view of an exemplary secular liberal like Richard Rorty. See *Contingency, Irony, and Solidarity* (Cambridge: Cambridge University Press, 1989); and also the treatment of Rorty's views offered in M. A. Casey, *Meaninglessness: The Solutions of Nietzsche, Freud and Rorty* (Lanham, MD: Lexington, 2001), chapter 3.

26. John Paul II, Encyclical Letter *Evangelium vitae* (1995), §70.

democracy is perfect or all wise. Indeed it has been said that democracy is the worst form of government except all those other forms that have been tried from time to time."[27] The legitimacy of a democracy, as of any form of government, stands or falls on whether it serves the common good, and does so well. Good democracy cannot simply be the acceptance of what the majority "considers moral and actually practices": would crimes cease to be crimes if, "instead of being committed by unscrupulous tyrants, they were legitimated by popular consensus?"[28] Clearly democracy is not a substitute for morality. But it is an excellent version of government—if people are educated in good judgment about citizenship values and a healthy respect for the common good.

Talk of the nature of democracy may sound suspicious to some liberal ears and consciences, but it proceeds from a deep respect for democracy and a wish to protect democracy's own ends and to stop it turning into simple majoritarianism. Thus the Catholic community claims the right to democratic input in two major ways: first, to speak up as one of the voices that respect democracy itself and want to see democracy flourish, grow in moral legitimacy, and not descend into a majority consensus based on short-termism or selfishness; and secondly, to contribute our own Christian views on all serious topics, as we have a democratic right and duty (as well as a divine mandate) to do. This is done differently by priests and bishops on the one hand, and Christian lay people more directly and regularly involved in political life on the other.

The best solution to conflicts and disagreements about rights is a moral realism that takes natural rights grounded on moral truths seriously. The best hope for achieving such a realism today is by insisting on genuine democracy, democracy legitimated by serious thought about the common good and basic human rights for every person, on our own shores and beyond. Where true democ-

27. Sir Winston Churchill, *Hansard*, 11 November 1947.
28. *Evangelium vitae*, §§69 & 70.

racy breaks down—where human rights are undermined by attacks on defenseless life, on the family, or on social justice in the name of ideology or party—the Church reserves the right to speak up for the democratic spirit, for the common good, and for the view of human rights based on the moral truth about the person.

CONCLUSION

From the time of St. John's Gospel, with its clash of light and darkness, godliness and "the world,"[29] Christians have realized that no earthly society is entirely congenial to living the Gospel.

Christian and Catholic life in Australia faces unique opportunities as well as particular challenges. Most Australians are Christians, but less than a quarter worship regularly.[30] Practice rates in the U.S.A. are much higher,[31] but so are the civic restraints on church practices and institutions there, and secular hostility to religion. The situation in Western Europe is particularly dire: low rates of attendance, strong secular hostility, and an adverse demographic situation.

Christian notions of regular religious worship and of mar-

29. See, for example, Jn. 15:18–19: "If the world hates you, be aware that it hated me before it hated you. If you belonged to the world, the world would love you as its own. Because you do not belong to the world, but I have chosen you out of the world—therefore the world hates you."

30. The 2002 Australian Wellbeing and Security Survey found that 24 percent of Christians worship once a month or more frequently. The 2001 National Church Life Survey estimated that 1.5 million Australians attended church on any given Sunday (8 percent of the 2001 population of 18.972 million), and probably twice that number attended within a given month.

31. Weekly church attendance in the United States is regularly reported to range from 40 percent upward, but since the late 1990s some studies have suggested that there may be a significant difference between the actual level of attendance and the level of attendance that people report to investigators. These studies suggest that actual weekly attendance may be in the order of 25 percent of the population, significantly lower than the usual figures of 40+ percent, but still significantly higher than weekly attendance in Australia. Measuring attendance in the United States as it is measured in Australia, namely, *monthly* or more frequently, would simply underscore this point. See Pippa Norris and Ronald Inglehart, *Sacred and Secular: Religion and Politics Worldwide* (Cambridge: Cambridge University Press, 2005), 89–92.

riage and family life are under pressure in most Western countries. The equilibrium regulating the number of children and sexual activity over the past fifty to one hundred years has been gravely disturbed by the invention of the contraceptive pill, women's liberation, the decline of religion, the separation of love, sexual activity, and children one from the other, and rising expectations of material prosperity. This has meant that no Western country produces sufficient children to keep the population stable, foreshadowing in some places long-term population decline.[32] Children are seen less as a gift from God and often as an expensive burden. Other crucial issues of social justice, euthanasia, and legalizing same-sex marriages surround this central challenge.

The quality of the Christian and Catholic response to these challenges will determine not only the future level of religious vitality in the Catholic community, but how much and for how long the Western world remains basically Christian.

32. See "The Role of the Bishop in Promoting the Gospel of Life" in this volume.

5. IS THERE ONLY
SECULAR DEMOCRACY?

IMAGINING OTHER POSSIBILITIES
FOR THE THIRD MILLENNIUM

One of the great vices of our age is that we get used to things too quickly. The German philosopher Nietzsche, a master of the dubious aphorism, once remarked that what does not kill us makes us stronger. He held that this was how we know that "someone has *turned out well.*"[1] For most of us, however, and for most of human history, it is truer to say that what does not kill us we learn to live with. Those of a more pessimistic bent than myself are even tempted to claim that there is nothing that human beings cannot accommodate themselves to, whatever their personal misgivings or fears might be in a given instance.

The course of democratic life in the West over the past forty years seems to bear this out. Television is a handy barometer of this. In recent times one very popular American daytime television show ran a program interviewing people whose intimate partners are animals, including a man who spoke of his five-year relationship with a horse called Pixel.[2] It is not the whole story of contemporary television, of course, and against this example we have to put shows like

This chapter was originally an address to the Annual Dinner of the Acton Institute for the Study of Religion and Liberty, Grand Rapids, Michigan, 12 October 2004. Subsequently published in the United States in *Journal of Markets and Morality* 7:2 (Fall 2004): 321–33, and in Australia in *Quadrant* 48:12 (December 2004): 8–13.

1. Friedrich Nietzsche, *Ecce Homo* (1908), in *The Anti-Christ, Ecce Homo, Twilight of the Idols and Other Writings*, ed. Aaron Ridley and Judith Norman, trans. Judith Norman (Cambridge: Cambridge University Press, 2005), 76–77.

2. Harry Stein, "Daytime Television Gets Judgmental," *City Journal*, Spring 2004 (www.city-journal.org).

Judge Judy, to name only one, which rate just as well and, whatever their shortcomings, make it very clear that bad behavior—even on television—should not be rewarded. But that daytime television should cover bestiality in the same way as it might cover a school's Fourth of July celebrations does not really cause us much surprise. This is a long way from the first night of television in Australia in 1956, when the comperes wore tuxedos and it was unthinkable—literally impossible to imagine—that the f-word would become a staple of dialogue in adult television dramas.

Other more important examples could also be given. Today Catholic teaching on artificial contraception is incomprehensible not only to secularists and some other Christians, but also to many Mass-going Catholics. It is not that the teaching is unreasonable or difficult to understand, but something more fundamental: many people do not see why the Church should insist on treating contraception as a moral issue of any sort at all. But forty years ago, prior to the United States Supreme Court decision in *Griswold v. Connecticut*, many American states had laws prohibiting or restricting contraception, and opponents of these laws had failed in every attempt they had made to have them overturned or diluted, both in the courts and in the legislatures. Even in the midst of the sexual revolution the state of New York continued to ban the sale of contraceptives to minors until 1977, when the Court struck the law down.[3]

Treating artificial contraception as morally objectionable is now considered one of those strange Catholic things, like devotion to the Infant of Prague. Only a little more than a generation ago, however, there was nothing strange about Catholic teaching in this area at all, because it was just one part of a wider moral consensus. It was from this consensus that laws against contraception arose. They were not the result of a conspiracy to keep the population ignorant and progenitive, but of democratic deliberation, debate, and decision.

3. Russell Hittinger, "Abortion before Roe," *First Things* 46 (October 1994): 14–16.

The same is true in the case of abortion. Attempts to repeal or liberalize anti-abortion laws, sometimes entailing referenda, were defeated by large majorities in most American states prior to the Supreme Court's decision in *Roe v. Wade*. These voters were the same people who voted against racial discrimination and for civil rights measures in the 1960s.[4] Since *Roe v. Wade* there have been, by one count, more than 40 million abortions performed in the United States.[5] The numbers in Australia are not quite so great, because we are a much smaller country, but proportionately they are just as alarming—averaging out at approximately ten abortions for every twenty-nine live births, one of the highest rates in the world.[6]

We have got used to this too—or at least, large numbers of our compatriots have. Whereas not so long ago abortion was prohibited and reprobated, politicians today who query the rate of abortion and the suffering it causes, as the federal minister of health in Australia has on several occasions in 2004, are treated as suspect, if not dangerous; and nominees to judicial office in the United States run the risk of being disqualified if they betray any pro-life convictions or sympathies.[7] This is despite the indications that, a generation on from the liberalization—or abolition—of the law in this area, growing numbers of people are uneasy about the accommodation democracy has made with abortion.

The point of these comparisons of now and then is not to indulge in nostalgia for how things used to be, or to suggest that ev-

4. Ibid.
5. Larry L. Eastland, "The Empty Cradle Will Rock," *Wall Street Journal*, 28 June 2004 (reprinted from *American Spectator*, June 2004).
6. There are approximately 90,000 abortions performed in Australia each year. In 2005 there were 261,000 live births registered (Australian Bureau of Statistics, *Australian Demographic Statistics*, December 2005). In 2004 Australia's abortion rate was estimated to be the second highest among fourteen developed nations, with the U.S.A. having the highest rate (Statistics New Zealand, *Demographic Trends 2004*).
7. Cf. John Paul II, Encyclical Letter *Centesimus annus* (1991), §46: "Those who are convinced that they know the truth and firmly adhere to it are considered unreliable from a democratic point of view, since they do not accept that truth is determined by the majority, or that it is subject to variation according to different political trends."

erything was fine forty years ago and is dreadful today. Nor should they be taken to mean that I believe the best way to deal with moral and social problems is always to legislate against them. Christians are realists. We do not live in the past, and we understand there is no golden age available to us, at least not before the angel Gabriel sounds the trumpet. There is no room for nostalgia, no looking back once we have put our hand to the plough (cf. Lk 9:62). We work for the kingdom in the here and now, and in doing so we should keep in mind how Jesus praised the shrewdness of the unjust steward (Lk 16: 1–13), and his advice to be "as wise as serpents and as innocent as doves" (Mt 10:16). It would make things very easy if we could legislate for virtue, and some have been trying to do this ever since Calvinism or the French Revolution. But while there are some things that should or can be appropriately legislated, legislating to require virtue, as I will explain shortly, is not a regular Christian option.

The purpose of my observations about television standards, and the past and present situation on contraception and abortion, is to highlight the point that for secular militants today democracy, more than anything else, means that anything is possible. Freedom today, in its everyday sense, means the limitlessness of possibility: whatever you want, whatever you like, you can do it. This is nonsense, of course. A moment's reflection on any number of "possibilities" reminds us that they are impossibilities. The American sociologist Philip Rieff has written of the important part that culture plays in creating a basic resistance to possibility, something within us that can give a compelling answer when our desires and will ask us the question "why not?"[8] Compelling answers to this need for self-restraint, for delayed gratification, are in short supply. The resources secular democracy has for this purpose seem to be exhausted, in a sea of rhetoric about individual rights.

I use the term *secular democracy* deliberately, because democracy

8. Philip Rieff, *Fellow Teachers*, 3rd ed. (Chicago: University of Chicago Press, 1985), 67 et passim.

is never unqualified. We are used to speaking of "liberal democracy," which as currently understood is a synonym for secular democracy; in Europe there are (or were) parties advocating "Christian democracy"; lately there has been much interest in the possibility of "Islamic democracy," and the shape it might take. These descriptors refer not simply to how democracy might be constituted, but to the moral vision democracy is intended to serve. This is true even, or especially, in the case of secular democracy, which some commentators—John Rawls, for example—insist is intended to serve no moral vision at all. In his encyclical letter *Evangelium vitae*, Pope John Paul II makes just this point when he argues that democracy "is a means and not an end. Its 'moral' value is not automatic," but depends on "the ends which it pursues and the means which it employs.... [T]he value of democracy stands or falls with the values which it embodies and promotes."[9] Democracy is not a good in itself. Its value is instrumental and depends on the vision it serves.

An attempt is sometimes made to evade this point by drawing a distinction between procedural democracy and normative democracy. Procedural democracy's claims are minimalist: democracy should be regarded as nothing more than a "mechanism for regulating different and opposing interests on a purely empirical basis." There is no doubt that this is part of what democracy should do, but as Pope John Paul II has pointed out, unless it is grounded in the moral law, the regulation of interests in participatory systems of government will occur "to the advantage of the most powerful, since they are the ones most capable of maneuvering not only the levers of power but also of shaping the formation of consensus." If democracy is only procedural, it "easily becomes an empty word."[10]

To speak of normative democracy, however, especially if one is a Catholic bishop, is to provoke panic in some quarters and de-

9. John Paul II, Encyclical Letter *Evangelium vitae* (1995), §70.
10. Ibid.

rision in others. Many things underlie this response, not least certain ideological convictions about secularism. But most important of all is a failure of imagination. George Weigel has pointed out the urgent need for a Catholic theory of democracy.[11] To some this can means theocracy, with bishops acting as party bosses and the citizenry being denied the opportunity to think or speak for themselves. To others it implies a contradiction in terms. Catholicism and freedom, it is assumed, cannot go together. In Richard Rorty's words, democracy is "an endless, proliferating realization of Freedom."[12] Making democracy Catholic or Christian would bring about the end of this proliferation. Democracy can be only what it is now: a constant series of "breakthroughs" against moral prejudice and social taboo in pursuit of the absolute autonomy of the individual.

Here we face a paradox. When it comes to self-realization, there is a mythology that there is almost nothing that cannot be done or desired. There are no limits to what we might will. But when it comes to how we should arrange our life in common and how we should order society and politics, we have only a very limited range of ideas. Over the course of history there have been monarchies of various sorts, republics of various sorts, dictatorships and tyrannies, and now secular democracy. What else can there be? It is impossible to imagine anything other than what we know now—except dictatorship. Limitless desire and limited imagination constitute another indication of the peculiar situation in which we find ourselves in the present age.

Think for a moment what it means to say that there can be no other form of democracy than secular democracy. Does democracy need a burgeoning pornography industry worth billions of dollars to be truly democratic? Does it need a rate of abortion that produces totals in the tens of millions? Does it need high levels of

11. George Weigel, "The Free and Virtuous Society: Catholic Social Doctrine in the Twenty-First Century," Fourth Annual Tyburn Lecture, Tyburn Convent, London, 19 May 2004.

12. Rorty, *Contingency, Irony and Solidarity*, xv–xvi.

divorce and marriage breakdown, with the growing rates of family dysfunction and individual suffering, especially for children and young people, that come with them? Does democracy need homosexual or polygamous relationships to be treated as the moral and functional equivalent of families based on monogamous marriage? And does it need these choices to be protected from any sort of public criticism? Does democracy (as in the case of Holland) need legalized euthanasia, extending to children under the age of twelve? Does democracy need assisted reproductive technology (such as in vitro fertilization) and embryonic stem cell research? Does democracy really *need* these things? What would democracy look like if you took many or all of these things out of the picture? Would it cease to be democracy? Or would it actually become more democratic?

These are the things by which secular democracy defines itself and stakes its ground against other possibilities. They are not merely epiphenomena of freedom of speech, freedom of thought, freedom of movement, freedom of opportunity, and freedom of choice. In most countries in the West they are not just options that may be taken. Increasingly they are the default position of the dominant forces of democratic social life, things from which one must opt out if one does not want to be part of them. The situation varies from place to place, of course, but many of the examples I have given are protected and sanctioned by law in most Western countries. The alarm with which sections of the media treat people in public life who are opposed to these things often implies that that they are a danger to democracy. This overreaction is of course a bluff, an attempt to silence opposition, almost suggesting that these practices, reprehensible to me, are necessary for secular democracy.

But what would democracy lose from dramatically lower rates of abortion or divorce? How would it be diminished if there were some successful controls in place on pornography, or if marriage was properly promoted and protected over other forms of relationship? Would democracy be poorer or more insecure if we had less family breakdown, leading on to lower rates of juvenile crime and welfare problems? Would young men and women really be disenfranchised if they were freed from the obligation to sleep with anyone they happen to go out with? Is the "right" of children under twelve to be euthanized what sets democracy apart from other forms of government? Does science in democratic countries need to insist on the manufacture and destruction of embryonic life for research purposes?

If we think about the answers to these questions, we begin to have an inkling about what a form of democracy other than secular democracy might look like. Having a name for this alternative form of democracy would obviously be useful. While "Catholic democracy" has some slight appeal for me personally, I do not think it would help us to corner the market. For the same reason "Christian democracy" should be passed over as well. Taking a leaf from the Pope John Paul II's work in this area, I would like propose that we call it *democratic personalism*.[13] It means nothing more than democracy founded on "the transcendent dignity of the human person." Placing democracy on this basis does not mean theocracy. It does not mean legislating for virtue. It does not mean the seizure of power by religious fundamentalism. Christian truth is not an ideology. It "does not presume to imprison changing socio-political realities in a rigid schema." Instead "it recognizes

13. Democratic personalism should be distinguished from *personalist democracy*, which Jacques Maritain promoted in the wake of the Second World War (and which inspired the European Christian Democratic parties) as an alternative to both radical individualism and totalitarianism. Rather than seeing democracy as one possible means of realizing the common good, Maritain came close to reading democracy off from the concepts of divine authority and natural law. He tended to see democracy as a good in itself—as the final flowering of the demands and values of the Gospel in the political realm, and as the end to which the social and political history of the West has progressed after long years of turbulence and injustice. His argument for democracy as the best possible regime—and possibly the only one consistent with the transcendent dignity of the person—strains the ancient and medieval sources, and goes further than the Church itself—or Pope John Paul II—have gone. See for example Jacques Maritain, *Christianity and Democracy* (1943), in *Christian Democracy and The Rights of Man and Natural Law*, trans. Doris C. Anson (San Francisco: Ignatius Press, 1986).

that human life is lived in history in conditions that are diverse and imperfect"; and because it constantly reaffirms the transcendent dignity of the person its method "is always that of respect for freedom."[14] As the Russian writer Victor Serge once remarked, ideology "can only impose its solutions by running people over." Christianity is not an ideology. It respects freedom. It does not offer programmatic "solutions," and it imposes itself on no one. It has to win majority support for any legislative measure proposed, to limit abuses and protect the public good.

Christianity proposes the truth about the human person. The foundations of secular democracy are coming to be seen as implausible, relying on the invention of "a wholly artificial human being who has never existed" and pretending that we are all instances of this species. "The pure liberal individual," as described by the English theologian John Millbank, is above all else characterized by the possession of will; "not a will determined to a good or even open to this or that, but a will to will." This concept of human nature, deriving from Rousseau and Hobbes, represents a complete repudiation of the transcendent dignity of the human person. The human individual is not "thought of as a creature, as a divine gift, as defined by his sharing-in and reflection-of, divine qualities of intellect, goodness and glory, but rather as a bare being." The only thing that distinguishes "this bare existence from a blade of grass or an asteroid" is its will, "which might be equally for good or for evil."[15] The "human experiences connected with love, family, friendship, church, citizenship, responsibility, and even death that make life worth living" are devalued and disregarded in pursuit of a frankly utopian vision of life freed from alienation and oppression through being "unconstrained by nothing but personal choice."[16] Secular democracy is democracy without transcen-

14. *Centesimus annus* §46.

15. John Millbank, "The Gift of Ruling: Secularization and Political Authority," *New Blackfriars* 996 (March 2004): 212–38, at 215.

16. Peter Augustine Lawler, "Communism Today," *Society* 41:4 (May–June 2004): 24–30, at 24.

dence, where the key point of reference is the supremacy of the individual and his unimpeded will.

At the level of lived experience, of normal day-to-day life, what has democracy without transcendence given us? Professor Jean Bethke Elshtain refers to the "mountain of data" from the social sciences showing that secular democracy in America today is "civically depleted, politically cynical and rootless, socially mistrustful and personally fearful."[17] She warns that "an anemic and faltering democratic faith—a decline of confidence in our basic institutions—threatens to render us incapable of sustaining these institutions over the long haul." She draws particular attention to the insistent denial of the proposition that "human life finds any point beyond itself,"[18] and how this undermines notions of the common good and the formation of character for democratic citizenship.[19] If democracy fundamentally means "the right to define one's own concept of existence, of meaning, of the universe, and of the mystery of human life,"[20] there can be no consensus about—perhaps even no conception of—the good life from which the development of individual character can take its orientation. The good life is something we make up or "define" for ourselves.

It is significant that Elshtain refers to the fearfulness that has crept into secular democracy. Terrorism has nothing to do with this, other than to amplify and provide a new focus—gated communities, after all, are not a post-9/11 phenomenon. One of the more interesting and important commentators writing in defense of secular democracy today is the English political philosopher John Gray. Gray takes fear as his point of departure. "The root of liberal thinking," he argues, "is not in love of freedom, nor in hope of progress, but in fear—the fear of other human beings." Democ-

---

17. Jean Bethke Elshtain, "Democratic Authority at Century's End," *Hedgehog Review* 2:1 (Spring 2000): 24–39, at 24.

18. Ibid., 36 (quoting Charles Taylor from an unpublished essay).

19. Ibid., 29.

20. *Planned Parenthood of South Eastern Pennsylvania* et al. v. *Casey, Governor of Pennsylvania*, et al. 505 US 833 (1992), at 851.

racy aims at nothing more than to deliver its subjects from death at the hands of their fellows. Gray's secular democracy is secular with a very small *s*.[21] In fact, he prefers to speak of "the liberal state," and repudiates the secularist expectation that the world's peoples and cultures will eventually converge in a universal civilization based on the absence of religion and the mania for rights.[22] His view of democracy is pragmatic and particularist—partly in an attempt to solve or evade the problem of finding a unifying moral consensus on which to place it. The state "is not the embodiment of a civil religion or a philosophy of history, nor the vehicle of a project of world-transformation, nor a means of recovering a lost cultural unity, but rather an artifice whose purpose is peace." Democracy is only one means of pursuing this purpose, and it may not have universal applicability.[23]

Gray opens up the bleak logic that has run its course in secular democracy. At its heart is fear, and fearfulness is increasingly part of the experience of life within it. The pursuit of radical individual autonomy creates a "war of all against all," in the form of an increasingly ruthless assertion of self against others. The limitlessness of possibility in secular democracy is also the limitlessness of power. It is not a matter of state surveillance, although that is also becoming an issue as secularism seeks to impose through administrative and judicial means certain "enforceable understandings" on issues such as homosexuality.[24] More important perhaps

21. John Gray, "Two Liberalisms of Fear," *Hedgehog Review* 2:1 (Spring 2000): 9–23, at 9–10.

22. Ibid., 22–23.

23. Ibid., 12–13. Gray seeks to manage the "divisive commitments" that arise in secular democracy by repudiating the requirement that they be privatized, and fostering instead "political institutions whose cultural identities are not singular, comprehensive, or exclusive (after the fashion of nineteenth-century nationalism and twentieth-century weltanschauung-states), but complex, plural, and overlapping" (ibid., 18–20). Like others before him he seems to believe that this "postliberal pluralism" will avoid degenerating into relativism, and moderate "the legalist culture of unconditional rights" that has been engendered by conflicts over values in democracy. But the example he gives of this new dispensation—the European Union—tends to discourage optimism.

24. Jean Bethke Elshtain, "The Bright Line: Liberalism and Religion," *New*

is the way this plays out "at the level of fundamental personal relations. Seeking at once to remain 'in control' and to evade the weakness and vulnerability that reliance on others entails, we conduct our most important relationships in a way conducive to high levels of anxiety, disappointment and hardness of heart." For when the individual is autonomous—alone able to determine when he will and will not be obligated to someone else—"being needed or dependent means being exposed to the power of others, especially the power of those closest to us."[25]

The social and political consequences are considerable. Family life becomes unstable, community begins to erode, regard for the common good becomes a secondary priority to the imperatives of self-realization. Perhaps most important of all is that people stop having children, or have only one or two. This is less of an issue in the United States compared to other Western countries, and there are reasons for this. All Western democracies have fertility rates below replacement level, including the United States—although at 2.0 births per woman per lifetime it is just below the replacement rate, unlike some European countries, which are dramatically below this level. The French demographer Jean-Claude Chesnais has drawn attention to the relationship between low birth rates and the temper of a culture. He argues that fertility will continue to decline until "there is a change of mood, . . . a shift from present pessimism to a state of mind which could be compared to that of the 'baby-boom' era." Chesnais argues that "the trivial interpretation of the baby-boom as a response to economic growth does not hold; the real crucial change was the change in the state of mind, from mourning to hope."[26]

Criterion 17:7 (March 1999): 4–13, at 12. For one interpretation of the imposition of "enforceable understandings" in the West, see "Thought Crime Becomes a Reality in Canada: An Interview with Michael O'Brien" (www.ignatiusinsight.com—reprinted from Our Sunday Visitor, 15 August 2004).

25. M. A. Casey, "Authority, Crisis, and the Individual," Society 39:2 (January–February 2002): 78–82, at 82.

26. Determinants of Below-Replacement Fertility. Expert group meeting on Below-Replacement Fertility, Population Division, Department of Economic and Social

Many things feed hope, especially lived Christianity. Love, courage, and trust are certainly part of the equation, but these virtues have to be fostered by the culture. They cannot flourish in a vacuum, or in a situation where radical individual autonomy disorders our most important relationships and disfigures life in common. When these conditions obtain, fear and confusion will be the consequence, and these work powerfully to undermine hope. Faith feeds hope too, not least by leading us out of disarray in relationships and mayhem in communities, and directing our efforts toward others. The recuperation of hope pays real social and human dividends, and "it is no accident"—as the Marxists used to say—that "there is a strong correlation between religious conviction and high fertility." In the West the people who are having children are people with faith.[27] If modernity and democracy mean secularism, then demography is against them.

Religious people have more children not because of mind control but because they have hope. Having children literally embodies confidence in the future and in the goodness of existence. Love is fruitful. It leads to life, and life in abundance. When we feel that we are part of a community where we are welcomed, where our contribution is valued, where we can take the risk of depending on others—and that the culture we are part of supports and protects these things—we embrace life and the future with a sense of expectation and trust. This is what hope means. Just as fear takes us to the heart of secular democracy, hope takes us to the heart of democratic personalism. We are now miles away from clichés about

Affairs, United Nations Secretariat, New York, 4–6 November 1997. Cited in Pontifical Council for the Family, *Declaration on the Decrease of Fertility in the World*, 27 February 1998.

27. Phillip Longman, *The Empty Cradle* (New York: Perseus Books, 2004), chapter 4. Longman uses the higher fertility rates of believers in an attempt to scare secularists into addressing the problem of subreplacement fertility. For example: "In a world of falling human population only fundamentalists would draw new strength. For the deep messages of the Bible and the Koran, and of all the world's ancient religions, are relentlessly pro-natal. And so, too, are the fundamentalist ideologies of fascism and racism" (at 5). Longman clearly sees this as a major threat to secularist democracy.

ONLY SECULAR DEMOCRACY? **81**

theocracy, and about Christianity being inherently anti-democratic. The difference between secular democracy and democratic personalism is the difference between democracy based on fear and democracy based on hope.

As Professor Elshtain reminds us, hope comes from transcendence, from the knowledge—not wishful thinking, but *knowledge*—that human life has a point beyond itself. The transcendent dignity of the person can be known from the fact "that we are stuck with living morally demanding lives" and that we cannot free ourselves from the experiences of alienation and meaninglessness through our own efforts.[28] In his great encyclical *Fides et ratio* Pope John Paul II showed how the search for truth, the need for belief, and dependence on others orients the individual—and human life in general—to transcendence.[29] These needs reflect the indivisible unity of freedom, reason, and love that constitutes human nature and sets us apart from all other creatures. Freedom is not merely "the will to will." Reason is not merely a form of instrumental intelligence, a sort of cunning that helps us get what our will wants. And love is not just a personal and private experience for the self. But if we regard them in isolation from each other and from the truth, as things that we possess rather than things we have been given, this is what they become. We turn in on ourselves and away from others, leaving ourselves nothing in the end but the comfort of carrion.

Transcendence directs us to our dependence on others and our dependence on God, and dependence is how we know the reality of transcendence.[30] There is nothing undemocratic about bringing this truth into our reflections about our social and political arrangements. "A genuinely human society flourishes when individu-

28. Lawler, "Communism Today," 29.
29. John Paul II, Encyclical Letter *Fides et ratio* (1998), §§28–33.
30. Ibid., §33: The individual's search "looks towards an ulterior truth which would explain the meaning of life. And it is therefore a search which can reach its end only in reaching the absolute. Thanks to the inherent capacities of thought, man is able to encounter and recognize truth of this kind. Such a truth—vital and necessary as it is for life—*is attained not only by way of reason but also through trusting acquiescence to other persons who can guarantee the authenticity and certainty of truth itself*" (emphasis added).

als dedicate the exercise of their freedom to the defense of others' rights and the pursuit of the common good, and when community supports individuals as they grow into a truly mature humanity."[31] To refound democracy on our need for others, and our need to make a gift of ourselves to them, is to bring a whole new form of democracy into being. If we have difficulty grasping this it is because secularism itself has worked to undermine, "both in theory and in practice, at almost every level of society, . . . the intellectual capacity to understand any reasonable alternative to a modern or post-modern understanding of man's purpose in being."[32]

Democratic personalism, basing social and political life on the transcendent dignity of the person, is perhaps the last alternative to secular democracy still possible within Western culture as it is presently configured. From outside Western culture come other possibilities, in particular that of Islam. It is still very early in the piece, of course, but the small but growing conversion of native Westerners within Western societies carries the suggestion that Islam may provide in the twenty-first century the focus and attraction that Communism provided in the twentieth, both for those who are alienated or embittered on the one hand, and for those who seek order or justice on the other. We assume that Western individualism and Islam are antithetical. In a context of personal and social disorder, it is not such a very great leap to make from the sovereignty of the individual's will to the sovereignty of God's will, loosely defined in many areas. In fact this could be a much easier transition than the transition from seeing oneself as supreme to seeing oneself as dependent on God and Christian constraints.

So alternatives are required. "If today there is a problem with

---

31. Weigel, "The Free and Virtuous Society."

32. James V. Schall, S.J., "The Culture of Modernity and Catholicism," *Homiletic and Pastoral Review* (June 2007), 10. See also Lawler, "Communism Today," 29: "The resources human beings have been given to live well as self-conscious mortals are love, virtue, and spiritual life, and the main effect of modern ideology has been to deprive human beings of the words or the self-understanding required to see this truth."

the recrudescence of intolerant religion," this is not a problem that secular democracy can resolve, but rather a problem that it tends to engender.[33] The past century provided examples enough of how the emptiness within secular democracy can be filled with darkness by political substitutes for religion.[34] Democratic personalism provides another, better possibility, one that does not require democracy to cancel itself out. It is based on a reading of modernity alternative to the secular reading that we are used to, and it has been provided by Pope John Paul II. Democratic personalism does not mean seizing power to pursue a project of world transformation, but broadening the imagination of democratic culture so that it can rediscover hope, and reestablish freedom in truth and the common good. It is a work of persuasion and evangelization, more than political activism. Its priority is culture rather than politics, and the transformation of politics through revivifying of culture. It is also about salvation—not least of all the salvation of democracy itself.

33. Millbank, "The Gift of Ruling," 235.
34. Ibid., 233.

FAITH, REASON, & LIFE

6. GOD, EVOLUTION, & CONSILIENCE

The distinguished Harvard University biologist Edward O. Wilson is highly regarded and is the recipient of many awards and fellowships. He has authored two Pulitzer Prize–winning books, *On Human Nature* (1978) and *The Ants* (1990), and his later book *Consilience: The Unity of Knowledge* was widely read and discussed when it appeared in 1998.

Wilson took the term *consilience* from an 1840 book of W. Whewell, an English philosopher of science, and used it to mean a linking of theories and facts across disciplines to create a single groundwork of explanation. The basics of his system are beguilingly simple: "Consilience holds that nature is organized by simple universal laws of physics to which all other laws and principles can eventually be reduced."[1] He is therefore a scientific materialist who believes "nothing fundamental separates the course of human history from the course of physical history."[2] As a consequence, human beings cannot be the center or summit of the universe,[3] and human rationality, self-consciousness, and intentionality are incidental rather than fundamental to the universe.

It is hazardous for a Catholic archbishop to review a book on evolution for a number of conflicting reasons. Most educated people know of the Inquisition placing Galileo under house arrest before his death in 1642, and of Pope John Paul's apology in 1992 for the Church's error. However, many might not realize that

---

This chapter was originally an address to the University Professors Program, Boston University, 23 September 1998, and subsequently was published in *The Australian's Review of Books*, December 1998.

1. Edward O. Wilson, *Consilience: The Unity of Knowledge* (New York: Alfred A. Knopf, 1998), 55.
2. Ibid., 11.
3. Ibid., 248.

88 FAITH, REASON, & LIFE

Copernicus was a priest who dedicated his work *On the Orbits of the Heavenly Bodies* (1543) to the pope and lived and worked unmolested by the Church.

Similarly, most would have heard of that famous occasion in 1860 when an ungentlemanly exchange took place in Oxford between Bishop Wilberforce and Thomas Huxley, who coined the term "agnostic," on the Darwinian hypothesis. We are told the bishop asked Huxley whether he was descended from an ape on his mother's or his father's side. Like much in the science–religion debate, elements of this story need to be taken with a pinch of salt: Bishop Wilberforce was in fact a respected scientist, a vice president of the British Academy, who made some careful criticisms of Darwin's formulations that were gratefully received. I cannot pretend to Wilberforce's scientific credentials—though I too am sufficiently disreputable in my academic background to have researched the likes of Origen, de Chardin, and Kohlberg, as well as the classics of philosophy and theology. However, experts in science and theology need to acknowledge the professional expertise and provenance of the other before thrashing out the proper relationship of the two.

If we want a symbol of the proper relationship of science to religion, let us not adopt examples such as Galileo or the human experimentation of the Nazis, which show religion and science at their worst or most foolish, but examples that show them at their best: perhaps the marvels of medical science and what it has made possible for human development in the postwar years; or further back in time, Pope Gregory XIII altering, despite opposition, the calendar in 1582 to align it with the true movement of the earth. This lead to the disturbance of rents and taxes and caused riots in Frankfurt over the ten "lost days." England came into line only in 1753, by which time eleven days had to be "lost," which also caused riots. Voltaire observed that "the English mob preferred their calendar to disagree with the Sun than to agree with the Pope."[4]

4. David Ewing Duncan, *The Calendar* (London: Fourth Estate, 1998), 307.

Naturally, I prefer Wilson's ideal of knowing everything over the nihilist and postmodernist view that we can know nothing, and I welcome his suggestion that we should solve the age-old debate between science and religion not by giving the victory to either side but by demonstrating the unity of the two. However, what I disagree with is his program for unity: at the end of the day, he believes unity will be achieved only if modern science dominates our world picture. There are some reasons why this is not a realistic nor a desirable goal.

REASON, ETHICS, AND DESIGN

In many ways Wilson's project is not an original one. The itch for comprehensiveness, the belief in "consilience," is one of the gifts of Christianity, first to the Roman world, and then to later worlds. Picking up on Aristotle's heroic attempts to unify all branches of knowledge (as later, Islamic and Jewish thinkers did too), Christian thinkers used the resources of the new disciplines of theology and Christian philosophy to take a cosmic position on topics generally treated parochially, including ethics, politics, even science. The notion of one worldview that can, ultimately, explain all phenomena is something we ponder largely because of the legacy of thinking on the monotheistic God, what George Steiner called "the brain-hammering strangeness of the monotheistic idea," and all that idea entails.[5]

As long as our theorizing is aimed at showing the coherence of truth and the consistency of all branches of knowledge, it is compatible with the Church's teaching and to be welcomed. However, there are hidden dangers in so grand an aim. In our tradition the first biologist was Adam, who was authorized to name all living things; tragically, he and his wife aspired to a divine omniscience and as a result saw their efforts to understand everything come to grief. The moral is that the laudable aims of unity and coherence

5. George Steiner, *In Bluebeard's Castle* (London: Faber and Faber, 1971), 36.

of knowledge can lead to the presumption of omniscience—the right to speak with equal authority on science, philosophy, the arts, social science, religion: the lot—and this is fraught with danger.

Wilson's heroes are the great Enlightenment figures—Smith, Hume, Kant, Voltaire, Haydn, and Mozart—and undoubtedly some fine work was done in that period. But the desire to explain everything also led to a growth in materialist reductionism. The idea that there is only one sort of causality (physical cause and effect) is rejected by the Church—not because the Church has any problem with the authority of science but because it believes that to reduce truth, goodness, and beauty to purely physical states of affairs is actually to distort the phenomena one is trying to explain. And this is the key to my position on evolution: of course the evolutionary hypothesis is almost certainly true and a fundamentalist creationist picture scientifically untenable, but evolution cannot account for all that we believe about the world and our place in it. It is much better at explaining how the colors of butterflies' wings change than explaining how butterflies developed. Some account of the relationship between religion and ethics on the one hand and evolution theory on the other might demonstrate this.

The sociobiological view of religion is that, at its best, it is about benevolence, altruism, human rights, upholding justice and mercy, maintaining hope, and the like. In other words, its province is exclusively human sentiments, tastes, useful virtues, and civilized values. However, this is to ignore the fact that religions such as Christianity also make certain truth-claims: truth-claims not only about morality but also about faith; for example, as a Catholic I believe that God created the universe, that Christ is the Son of God, and that his sacrifice on the cross made everlasting life a possibility for every human being. For me, it is Christian teaching and the power of reason that provide some escape from the pressures of the unknowable and the inevitable. Now, one may think that to assert these propositions is a matter of misplaced sentiment or plain delusion, but the fact is that these alleged truth-claims have to be taken on their own terms as truth-claims. Naturally, they are just as open to challenge and rational debate as any other truth-claims, but the point is that they are propositional in form: they cannot be set aside as "obviously" emotional, or as strategies for self-interest and survival. As with any other propositional claims made in the course of an argument, they must be either accepted or disproved—and rational disproof of the foundational claims of Christianity is a very difficult task (consider the best efforts from the Enlightenment to Marx, and the paradoxical growth in religious belief during this "period of unbelief"). One therefore can ask Professor Wilson to take seriously the claims religion makes, on their own terms, before beginning the process of reducing them to genetics and evolutionary forces.

This is not to take issue with evolution theory. God is not a scientific hypothesis that might rival evolution. To think he is reduces the Creator to a creature, a highly creative force within the universe. God is not an occupant of the universe at all, but an answer to the question "why is there a universe?" God and many concepts of evolution can exist quite happily. In fact, a good case can be made out that evolutionary theory actually needs the hypothesis of God for completeness. Let me say a little more about this, specifically in terms of our moral and other values.

Many values and virtues we cherish do not make sense in evolutionary terms: for example, the totally exceptionless prohibitions absolute morality places upon certain heinous and degraded acts. Other values, such as forgiveness, pity, altruistic sentiments, and universal justice, must be falsified—described as other than they actually are—in order to fit in with the theory. One may not agree with this morality, but the point is: many people do agree, and it seems impossible in evolutionary terms to account for such things as universalism in ethics.

Now, some would argue: acting toward strangers with impartial justice or costly mercy does ultimately serve to benefit oneself or one's kin, for it adapts our social environment so that it is better suited toward the survival of us all. Thus Matt Ridley has argued that we have evolved innate dispositions toward cooperation, tribal thinking, and reciprocal altruism that account for moral behavior. We (or our kin, those close to us) gain more than we lose by such behavior.[6] This theory construes morality as competition and virtue as the skill to see that winning requires consensus and contract. Obviously Ridley is not claiming this is how individual agents actually think, but my criticism is that he has not fully accounted at all for the central propositions morality upholds. For instance, justice, integrity, and love are fundamental human values not just because they have proved useful in the evolutionary struggle. Similarly, no alternative facts about evolutionary history could have made pack-rape or child molestation good: they cannot be good even if accompanied by human benefits. Even if they would procure the survival of the human race, such acts would remain evil because of what they are—and with more argument than I can give, similar points could be made about the other central human (and they are human, not just Christian) virtues and values.

Now, this position is not solely that of the Catholic Church. The radical incompleteness of evolution theory is increasingly apparent to many philosophers as well as theologians. In his book *Beyond Evolution*, Anthony O'Hear, professor of philosophy at Bradford, argues that despite its success in the natural world, evolution cannot explain our pursuit of the truth, our striving to become and to do good, or our appreciation of beauty. These are activities quite fundamental to human flourishing and well-being and often practiced, argues O'Hear, to the detriment of our survival, our reproduction, or the interests of our fellows.[7]

O'Hear's conclusion—that our rationality equips us, uniquely, to surpass our evolutionary inheritance—is also shared by Thomas Nagel, a major U.S. philosopher, himself no believer, who argues that "the idea that our rational capacity was the product of natural selection would render reason . . . less trustworthy. . . . There would

6. Matt Ridley, *The Origins of Virtue: Human Instincts and the Evolution of Cooperation* (London: Penguin, 1998). Review by Frank J. Sulloway, "Darwinian Virtues," *New York Review of Books*, 9 April 1998, 34–40.

7. Anthony O'Hear, *Beyond Evolution* (Oxford: Clarendon Press, 1997).

be no reason to trust its results in mathematics and science, for example. (And insofar as the evolutionary hypothesis itself depends on reason, it too would be self-undermining)."[8] Nagel is in no way denying natural selection. His claim is that it is incomplete. In particular, it cannot account for rationality and for all our rationality can accomplish, especially logical, scientific, and moral-spiritual thinking. Therefore, it is a misconception to see this as only a debate between believers and nonbelieving evolutionists: many nonbelievers too would criticize natural selection—for example, for not acknowledging purpose.

However, my position is not only that evolution leaves reason and ethics unexplained, but also that evolution requires the hypothesis of an intelligence at the center of the universe—a hypothesis far more likely to be true than any of the tortuous attempts to replace it made in the last two centuries. Wilson himself claims to "lean towards deism," "towards a cosmological God who created the universe" but is excluded from directing organic evolution.[9] Such a god does not provide the sort of ongoing involvement with creation that is needed. As John Haldane, professor of philosophy at St Andrews, explains: "Evolutionary theory, and naturalism more generally, are not equipped to explain three important differences which common sense and philosophically unprejudiced science both recognize: those between the inanimate and the animate; the non-reproductive and the reproductive; and the non-mental and the mental. Assuming a history of development, these differences involve a series of ascents giving rise to explanatory gaps in evolutionary theory."[10]

Haldane's point is that evolution was, and is, a process, and within this process there repeatedly appear gaps so vast that natural forces operating alone could not cross them. The steps from

8. Thomas Nagel, *The Last Word: Philosophical Essays* (Oxford: Oxford University Press, 1997), 135.

9. Wilson, *Consilience*, 241.

10. J. J. C. Smart and J. J. Haldane, *Atheism and Theism* (Oxford: Blackwells, 1996), 119.

lifeless matter to living things, and from living things to living things that are self-conscious, think, communicate, and make moral judgments are not just increases in the degree of physical complexity: they are historical developments of new sorts of complexity in the universe. The impersonal, indifferent God of the deists is unavailable to explain why or how these steps to life, consciousness, and reason occur. For Wilson, the patterns and laws he describes in encyclopedic detail are without purpose. The dazzling, baffling harmony of evolution has at its core less sense of purpose than a chimpanzee.[11] The universe is pattern without purpose.

Of course, nonbelievers will be unwilling to appeal to God to account for alleged gaps in the evolutionary story, but this unwillingness requires a rational case against God, not just setting him aside as an inconvenient or unloved hypothesis. It is interesting to reflect on the famous passage in Darwin's autobiography where he speaks of "the extreme difficulty or rather impossibility of conceiving this immense and wonderful universe ... as the result of blind chance or necessity. When thus reflecting ... I deserve to be called a theist." Darwin, of course, went on to say that he always ends by distrusting this recurrent thought since he considers all thoughts to be evolution-based.[12] But why was the thought there? How does evolutionary theory account for the fact that most people in history have believed in God or in gods? Why might blind nature have so protected us from the abyss and the pressures of meaninglessness and despair?

Some may answer "to help us survive." But why should we need to be protected from the knowledge that everything comes down to survival? If the evolutionary story were the whole truth, we should have settled by now into accepting survival as a satisfactory substitute for God; but we have not, and that is telling. We should also acknowledge that the explicit recognition of purpose

11. Cf. Wilson, Consilience, 133.
12. Gavin de Beer, ed., Charles Darwin and Thomas Huxley: Autobiographies (New York: Oxford University Press, 1974), 54.

or design in nature takes most people one dangerous step closer toward acknowledging an intelligent Designer "behind" the whole of nature.

The case for design has been brilliantly stated by Michael J. Behe.[13] The new field of biochemistry, which blossomed after Watson's and Crick's discovery of the structure of DNA, has revealed a world of staggering complexity. The professional literature is silent on how gradualistic Darwinian evolution might have produced the dazzling structure of finely calibrated, interdependent parts necessary, for example, for vision or blood-clotting.

Because Crick believes that the undirected origin of life is a virtually insurmountable obstacle, he thinks life on earth may have begun when aliens sent a rocket-ship with spores to seed the earth![14] It is therefore not surprising that Sir Hans Kornberg, another distinguished British biologist, formerly professor of biochemistry and Master of Christ's College at Cambridge University, remarked that for scientists, teleology is like a lady of ill-repute. Nobody wants to be seen with her in public, but many use her at night.[15] Another professor of biology claims that scientists in the future will look back on Neo-Darwinism as "a minor twentieth century religious sect."[16]

13. Michael J. Behe, *Darwin's Black Box: the Biochemical Challenge to Evolution* (New York: Free Press, 1996).

14. For Crick's often-published belief in aliens as the source of life on earth, see ibid., 248. As Behe explains, "the primary reason Crick subscribes to this unorthodox view is that he judges the undirected origin of life to be a virtually insurmountable obstacle, but he wants a naturalistic explanation."

15. Remarks made to the author by Professor Kornberg at Boston University, 23 September 1998.

16. Professor Lynn Margulis quoted in Behe, *Darwin's Black Box*, 26. Margulis is Distinguished University Professor of Biology at the University of Massachusetts. Behe writes that "at one of her many public talks she asks the molecular biologists in the audience to name a single unambiguous example of the formation of a new species by the accumulation of mutations. Her challenge goes unmet." Ibid.

ORDERS OF INTELLIGIBILITY

As a framework for understanding how evolution is compatible with the existence of God we can distinguish, following Aquinas at the beginning of his Commentary on Aristotle's *Ethics*, the physical order of causes and effects; the mental order of concepts; the existential order of choices and acts; and the cultural order of making what is useful and beautiful.[17]

For example, take our knowledge of human beings: we know much about them that is purely physical, but also much that cannot be explained at the physical-evolutionary level. It is not because it is useful for evolutionary purposes that we value truth, goodness, and beauty. Even if our evolutionary survival required it, we could not make true propositions false, wicked acts good, useless objects valuable, or beautiful objects trash, and we would be repelled by the suggestion that we should so deceive ourselves. The laws of logic and ethics that govern these things are just as irreducibly basic as the laws of physics. If we reduced science to the existential order—made it all a matter of ethics or religion—we would do a great disservice to science and actually lose sight of the natural phenomena it seeks to explain. Similarly, to reduce ethics and religion to the physical order is to lose the very values and norms ethicists and archbishops uphold.

Naturally all these orders are interrelated. Thus our capacities for moral and spiritual debate can be explained by the structure of our bodies and brains—as much that is done in science can be explained by fundamental ethical values, religious yearnings, logical principles, and artistic and technological purposes. But there is an irreducible core within each order that cannot be captured in a reductionist program. To acknowledge this is, for me, to begin to approach true consilience, the unity of knowledge.

Within my own field of religion it is disappointing that Wil-

17. See the opening of St. Thomas Aquinas, *Commentary on Aristotle's Nicomachean Ethics*, trans. C. I. Litzinger (Notre Dame, IN: Dumb Ox Books, 1993).

son, after expressing a desire to treat the strongest theology he could discover, settled for attacking some fairly standard positions. His own points too are not always well taken. That religious people have done wicked things is certainly no sort of evidence against God's existence. Indeed, wickedness is something the theist can fairly easily account for with his explanations of sin and original sin, which is not something that could be said of the evolutionist. Perhaps Wilson here is touched by Enlightenment optimism that with the fading of religion, oppression and injustice would cease. The Terror of the French Revolution at the end of the eighteenth century and both Nazism and Communism in our own times have disposed of that misconception. His view of religion as a sort of instinctual tribalism, or akin to a nonrational animal submissiveness, exhibits the sort of failure to take the propositional revelation mentioned earlier seriously and on its own terms. Nevertheless, Wilson is forced to acknowledge the fact that as science has progressed so has religion, with spiritual wisdom developing to moderate "barbaric tenets."[18] He believes, however, that science is the grander system and that it will one day replace religious narratives with a finer evolutionary narrative of its own. Even religion—perhaps especially religion—is subject to the imperialistic reductionism of the research laboratory in Wilson's vision. To hold that the story of purposeless cosmic evolution might one day provide an epic that will do for us what the Scriptures, the Koran, the life of Buddha currently do for billions seems to me what used to be called a "category mistake," with religion as the category that is misunderstood.

INTERNAL PROBLEMS

There are some final points I would like to make that are internal to Wilson's argument. First, he is clearly dazzled by the power of scientific materialism. In 1978 he wrote: "The time has come

18. Wilson, *Consilience*, 244.

to ask: Does a way exist to divert the power of religion into the service of the great new enterprise that lays bare the sources of that power? . . . Make no mistake about the power of scientific materialism. It presents the human mind with an alternative mythology that has until now, point for point in zones of conflict, defeated traditional religion."[19] There is a hint here of something Faustian in his project, a point he repeats in *Consilience* when he writes of the Faustian choices confronting us now.[20] This powerfulness contrasts with what is, or should be, the attitude of Christians to the cosmos: awe, reverence, wonder, respect. There seems to me to be the danger of a sort of presumption in using the insights of modern science to "power through" the secrets of the natural world. Ironically, then, Christians, who are often criticized for dogmatism and absolutism about many things, are committed to holding that the full explanation of the universe is not ours until we enter the Kingdom; to hope for more in this life was the sin of Adam and Eve and, I suggest, the original sin alive and kicking still in all of us.

Secondly, the actual definition of *consilience* is still worrying. Wilson defines it as "the linking of facts and fact-based theory across disciplines to create a common groundwork of explanation."[21] But what sort of links is it that are required? And just how do you link facts and theories? What is the criterion for "common"? Just how reductionist is his explanatory base? What is clear is that for Wilson it is only the methods of natural science that can establish or refute the links that will create unified understanding. Thus it seems to be not the unity of science with other disciplines but the dominance of science, especially the biological sciences, that he preaches. Surely what we require is a dialectic of science with art, ethics, the social sciences, and religion. Without this we risk a very adult science with very adolescent ethics, and this is something we cannot afford with new scientific breakthroughs in genetics and related fields announced every day.

19. Edward O. Wilson, *On Human Nature* (Cambridge, MA: Harvard University Press, 1978), 196.
20. Wilson, *Consilience*, 270.   21. Ibid., 9.

Thirdly, in a powerful and unfriendly review in the *New Republic*, Tzvetan Todorov has pointed out that Wilson has no place for human freedom.[22] Choice is a useful illusion; the capacity to believe passionately in free will is "a fortunate circumstance";[23] but in the future we shall understand more clearly how everything is the necessary effect of a physical cause or causes; how moral sentiments are the product of interaction between genes and environment. Presently, writes Wilson, we "lack a foundation of verifiable knowledge of human nature sufficient to produce cause and effect predictions."[24]

This is an example of what Todorov calls the "hard version" of Wilson's theory. Todorov also finds present a soft version, which acknowledges that physics does not adequately explain life, just as biology does not fully explain culture. Wilson also makes much of the present developing human capacity to take life in directions we choose; "volitional evolution" he calls it.[25] Todorov finds the coexistence of these two versions in the one book to be "logically untenable."

Fourthly, toward the end of the book Wilson makes some controversial points about biopessimism, the population disaster that, it is alleged, all "statured scientists" predict.[26] This pessimism is excessive, and unilateral, and the Ehrlichian view is surely widely challenged. The 1996 Revision of the UN Population Division's biennial compendium *World Population Prospects* included "low variant" projections for long-term population decline, with negative growth—depopulation—occurring after 2040, and the 2004 Revision confirmed this trajectory. In the same year as *Consilience* was published, the Pontifical Council for the Family produced a document calling for the full truth about demographic trends to be more widely known, and this call has been heeded to a large ex-

22. Tzvetan Todorov, "The Surrender to Nature," *New Republic*, 27 April 1998.
23. Wilson, *Consilience*, 120.
24. Ibid., 255.
25. Ibid., 273–77. See also 118–20 on free will.
26. Ibid., 280.

tent.[27] In 1996, 51 countries (out of 185), representing 44 percent of the world's population, were no longer able to replace their people. Eight years later, according to the 2004 Revision of the UN's *World Population Prospects*, the number of countries with subreplacement fertility had risen to 65 (including 22 developing countries), and their share of world population had fallen to 42.8 percent. The population implosion, the demographic winter, especially in the developed world, will bring vast changes, probably in the size of the workforce and in the value of pensions. If Italy's fertility rate of the late 1990s were to continue until 2050, three-fifths of Italian children will have no siblings, cousins, aunts, or uncles, while for Europe as a whole two-fifths of children would be in this situation.[28]

While there is no denying the general pressures on resources and from increasing population in some parts of the developing world, international data on the decrease in fertility shows it is now spreading from the industrial countries to developing nations in Asia and the Middle East. This highlights a particular nightmare of rapidly aging populations: whereas Western countries grew rich and then grew old, developing countries are growing old before they grow rich, making it less likely that they will ever do so.[29]

Edward Wilson advances a limited sort of salvation through science. In many ways the degree of fervor with which he writes suggests the craving of the overly atomistic modern world for the synthetic unity Christianity once gave Western thinkers. Wilson's double brand of consilience, hard and soft, extreme and moderate, is partly explained by the fact that Wilson believes more than he can demonstrate scientifically at this stage of knowledge. He is a true believer, but not in religion. For him there is no way to resolve

27. Pontifical Council for the Family, *On the Decrease of Fertility in the World*.
28. Nicholas Eberstadt, "Two Few People?" *Prospect* 25 (December 1997), 50–55.
29. See "The Role of the Bishop in Promoting the Gospel of Life" in this volume.

the contradictions between religious and intellectual truth, and he looks forward confidently to "the secularization of the human epic and religion itself."[30]

Attempts to show the harmony of truths are commendable but always chancy. However, to search for all-embracing unity while upholding a form of materialist reductionism seems to me to miss something important that monotheistic religions have always taught: that truth may be one from God's perspective, but it is many from ours. In other words, human discourse is necessarily multiform—and necessarily incomplete. That is why I think that what we contemplate in religion is eminently grander than the vision Wilson offers. Consilience, if it is possible at all, requires the God who has promised that one day we shall all know as we are known.

30. Wilson, *Consilience*, 265.

7. THE ROLE OF THE BISHOP IN PROMOTING THE GOSPEL OF LIFE

DECLINING BIRTH RATES

Oshima is a small Japanese island, thirty-two kilometers long, cradled between the large islands of Honshu, Shikoku, and Kyushu. There we can confront the future. In 2005, Japan had the oldest population in the world, because the Japanese are living longer and having fewer and fewer children. Their fertility rate fell to 1.33 in 2005, down from 1.39 in 2000 and well below the rate of 2.1 children per woman necessary to keep the population stable.[1]

Oshima is the Island of the Old, with the oldest population in the oldest country. When a Western journalist visited the island in 1999, the barber with the cutthroat razor was 84 years of age, as was the papergirl. The taxi driver was only 83 years old, and the policeman a sprightly 60 year-old. In the town of Towa, at the eastern end of the island, octogenarians outnumbered teenagers by more than three to one, septuagenarians by seven to one; half the population was over 65. Towa had a population of 20,600 in 1945; fifty-five years later the population was 5,500.[2]

Although the trends in Oshima have been worsened by youth

This chapter was originally an address to the Linacre Centre International Conference, Queens College, University of Cambridge, 5 July 2000. It was subsequently published in Luke Gormally, ed., *Culture of Life—Culture of Death: Proceedings of the International Conference on "The Great Jubilee and the Culture of Life"* (London: Linacre Centre, 2002). All statistics cited have been updated to the latest available in 2006 wherever possible.

1. United Nations Department of Economic and Social Affairs, Population Division, *World Population Prospects: The 2004 Revision* (2005).

2. Richard Lloyd Parry, "Old World Order," *Australian Magazine, Weekend Australian*, 8–9 January 2000.

emigration for work, Oshima is not a social aberration, a development that goes against the current. Following present patterns, Japan's population of 128 million will be reduced by *two-thirds* by the end of the twenty-first century[3]—and Europe's will be halved.[4]

Thirty years ago, when fears of uncontrollable population growth were at their height, the world's population had already commenced its long and steady slide to zero population growth and to the negative population growth—that is, depopulation—that lies beyond that point. In the decade from 1965 to 1975, world birth rates decreased by 13 percent, with decline occurring in 127 countries.[5] In 1996, and again in 2004, the United Nations forecast zero population growth for the world as a whole by 2040, with population peaking at 7.7 billion. World population would decline thereafter by 25 percent in each successive generation to yield an expected population in 2100 of 5.6 billion. This anticipated decline in population does not factor in the results of war, famine, environmental disaster, or epidemics (although the 2004 UN projections do take the AIDS epidemic into account).[6] It is

3. Official Japanese projections offer low, medium, and high variants, which put the country's estimated population in 2100 at 46.4 million, 64.1 million, and 81.7 million respectively. See National Institute for Population and Social Security Research, *Population Projections for Japan 2001–2050* (2003).

4. United Nations, Department of Economic and Social Affairs, Population Division, *World Population in 2300* (2004). In these UN studies projections are always given in the form of low, medium, and high variants. The low variants have been used in this paper, following the practice adopted in the expert commentary consulted in its preparation. The UN itself recommends the use of the medium variants, but describes each of the variants offered as "provid[ing] reasonable and plausible future trends."

5. Ron Brunton, *The End of the Overpopulation Crisis?* (Melbourne: Institute of Public Affairs, 1998), 16.

6. Since 1980, 25 million people have died from AIDS, and 65 million have been infected with HIV. Because of AIDS, life expectancy in southern Africa has fallen from 61 years in 1985–90 to 48 years in 2000–2005. Sub-Saharan Africa had 64 percent of all people infected with HIV in 2005 (down from 70 percent in 1999), and 2 million dead from the disease (up from 1.9 million in 2003). In Asia there were 930,000 new infections in 2005 (down from 1.4 million in 1999), and 8.3 million people living with HIV, more than two-thirds of them in India. HIV came relatively late to Papua New Guinea, but that country accounted for 90 percent of new

a product of a drastic fall in fertility that will unfold, to use the optimistic language of the UN document, "under conditions of orderly progress."[7]

This dramatic fall in birthrates is occurring in a context where people are living longer and longer, a corollary of the "health explosion" modern people are so fortunate to enjoy.[8] The combination of low fertility and longer lives will mean "a radical aging of the human population—a shift whose magnitude would be without historical precedent." In 1900 the global median age was about 20 years, not much more than what it had been in all other eras.[9] It had risen to just under 24 years by 1950, and by 2050 it will about 43 years. Italy, Germany, and Japan have the oldest populations in the world today, with median ages between 42 and 43. By 2050 however, the population of the less developed regions will have a median age of 41.7, while the median age of Italy and Japan will be over 58 and Germany's 53.2. South Korea will also rank as one of the oldest populations in the world in 2050, with a median age of 59.2 compared to 35 in 2005. The median age for the more developed regions of the world will be 51.5, while Europe's median age will be 53.3.[10]

An aging population will be an enormous problem for wealthy developed nations to deal with, but a problem of an altogether different magnitude for developing countries. The United States might worry about the impact of an aging population on its pension system, but China has no pension system to speak of, and by

---

infections in Oceania (excluding Australia and New Zealand) in 2005. UNAIDS, *2006 Report on the Global AIDS Epidemic* (2006).

7. United Nations, Department of Economic and Social Affairs, Population Division, *World Population Prospects: The 1996 Revision* (1997). See also *World Population Prospects: The 2004 Revision.* Since 1994, the estimates of total world population in 2050 have tended consistently downward, falling 0.3 billion, 0.8 billion, and 1.3 billion in the low, medium, and high variants respectively:

1994:	7.9 billion	9.8 billion	11.9 billion
2004:	7.6 billion	9.0 billion	10.6 billion

8. Peter G. Peterson, *Gray Dawn* (New York: Times Books, 1999), 41.

9. Eberstadt, "Too Few People?" 52.

10. *World Population Prospects: The 2004 Revision*, vol. 3: *Analytical Report*, chapter 2.

2050 almost 37 percent of its population will be aged 60 years or over, compared to just under 31 percent of the U.S. population. While the proportion of people 60 or older will double in Europe to over 40 percent by 2050 (and higher in many European countries), it will increase by 2.7 times in the Caribbean (to 29.7 percent), by 3.4 times in Brazil and Indonesia (to 30 and 28.6 percent respectively), and by 4.7 times in Iran (to 31 percent). It will also treble or more than treble in Thailand, Pakistan, Bangladesh, the Middle East, and India, although in every one of these except Thailand the proportion of the population over 60 will still be relatively lower than elsewhere, ranging from 18 to 25 percent. The impact of population aging will be greater in some of these countries, such as India and China, because of vast differences in wealth across regions.[11]

As recently as the late 1960s the world's total fertility rate—that is, the number of births per woman per lifetime[12]—was 4.9. In 2005 it stood at 2.6. In some developing countries, this decline has been more spectacular still. Mexico has dropped from 6.8 to 2.4; India from 5.7 to 3.1, Iran from 6.8 to 2.1, and China (with its brutally enforced "one-child norm"), from 6.0 to 1.7.[13] In the developed world the fall in total fertility rates has occurred over a longer period, and today every developed nation has a total fertility rate below the replacement rate of 2.1 (except Albania at 2.29). With a total fertility rate of 2.04 the U.S.A. is at the high end of the scale for the developed world, along with Ireland, Iceland, and New Zealand, each with a rate of 1.9 or so. In Japan, Germany, and Italy the rate is 1.3, in South Korea and most east or central European countries it is 1.2; Ukraine has the lowest fertility rate of any country at 1.1.[14] Rates below 1.0 have been recorded in some regions

11. *World Population Prospects: The 2004 Revision.*
12. The total fertility rate is generally considered a more reliable indicator than simple birth rates—numbers of children per 1,000 women—because the latter can be skewed by changes in the age distribution of women.
13. *World Population Prospects: The 2004 Revision.*
14. Ibid.

in Europe, including Saxony, Catalonia, the Basque country, Tuscany, and the regions around Rome and Venice.[15] Bologna recorded a fertility rate of 0.8 in 1997, and although it may have lifted slightly since then, it remains one of the lowest in Europe.[16]

As couples have only one or two children—or none at all[17]—the family itself will be drastically narrowed and lengthened in its shape. If the trends in those countries with the lowest fertility rates—Italy for example—continue, then within two generations more than three in every five children will have "neither brothers nor sisters, nor uncles nor aunts, nor cousins." Projecting the fertility rates of the European Union over two generations only slightly alters this scenario. "About 40 percent of European children would have no collateral blood relatives [and] less than one-sixth would have a brother or a sister and a cousin."[18] The genealogical tree "will be all stem and no branch."[19]

Contrary to some expectations, the economic and social problems caused by these enormous demographic changes are not ones that can be easily offset by increased immigration. The level of migration needed to offset population aging is extremely large, "and in all cases entails vastly more immigration than occurred in the past."[20] The UN estimates that to keep its total population at 1995 levels throughout the period to 2050, the EU alone would need

15. Allan C. Carlson, "Sweden and the Failure of European Family Policy," *Society* 42:6 (September–October 2005): 41–46, at 41 and 44.

16. Michael Specter, "Population Implosion Worries a Graying Europe," *New York Times*, 10 July 1998.

17. In 2000 it was estimated that if past patterns of childlessness applied to Australian women who have not yet completed their fertility, 24 percent would remain childless. Australian Bureau of Statistics, *Births, Australia 2000*. In 2001 it was estimated that 12.8 percent of Australian women complete their fertility with only one child, and 41 percent with only two. David de Vaus, *Diversity and Change in Australian Families: Statistical Profiles* (Melbourne: Australian Institute of Family Studies, 2004), 187.

18. Eberstadt, "Too Few People?" 55.

19. Peterson, *Gray Dawn*, 57.

20. United Nations, Department of Economic and Social Affairs, Population Division, *Replacement Migration: Is It a Solution to Declining and Aging Populations?* (2000).

949,000 migrants a year, compared to 857,000 a year between 1990 and 1998. This may not seem like an impossible goal, but even lifting annual immigration by 90,000 a year would not stop population aging. To keep the size of the working population (15–65 years old) stable throughout this period, annual immigration would almost have to double, to 1.588 million. But even that would not be enough. One measure of the age of a population is the ratio of working-age people to people aged 65 or over. In 1995 the EU ratio stood at 4.3 working-age people to 1 older person (in 1950 it was 7 to 1). To maintain this ratio from 1995 to 2050, 12.736 million immigrants would be required annually, which by the last ten years of this period would be equivalent to half the world's annual population increase.[21] It is not difficult to imagine the political problems that immigration at these sorts of levels will create even in the most enlightened and liberal Western countries.

In its 1998 declaration on the fall in fertility the Pontifical Council for the Family raised the question of how an increase in a population's mean age might affect its "psychological profile." "Moroseness," which the declaration describes as "the lack of intellectual, economic, scientific and social dynamism and reduced creativity," is likely to be a conspicuous feature of elderly societies, and may "already be at work" in those countries leading the trend.[22] In Australia depression is already a significant problem, costing $14.9 billion a year nationally, with more than 6 million working days lost annually, and treatment costs of $600 million.[23] The main author of a UN report on which the declaration draws, Jean-Claude Chesnais, director of research at the French National Institute for the Demographic Studies, puts this point simply: "You cannot have a successful world without children in it." This point is dramatically illustrated in P. D. James's novel *The Children of*

21. Ibid.
22. Pontifical Council for the Family, *Declaration on the Decrease of Fertility in the World*, 27 February 1998.
23. figures from the Australian Government's Department of Health and Ageing.

Men (1993), which is set in 2021 in a world that has not seen a child born for over a generation because of universal male sterility.[24]

The American social critic Gertrude Himmelfarb has also pointed out that almost certainly the family in the Western world will undergo a second revolution to deepen the impoverishment it has suffered after the first revolution that is "reflected in the statistics of divorce, illegitimacy, single-parenthood and cohabitation." "In addition to the fatherless family," Himmelfarb writes, "we now have to worry about a family without peers."[25] The family "has been the primary and indispensable instrument for socializing people," but in a world where the vast majority of children find themselves without brothers and sisters, cousins, uncles, or aunts, the "extended bonds of obligation and [the] reciprocal resources—including emotional resources" that play such an important part in a child's life and development will be enormously diminished. The nuclear family is sometimes criticized for its failings compared to earlier forms of family arrangement, but "the nuclear family does not begin to approach the limits of social atomization which may await us in a depopulating world."[26] Already in mainland China, with its ruthless one-child policy, there is concern over the long-term behavior of the "little princes," the pampered single sons this policy has produced in abundance.

This thumbnail sketch of family life in the Western world highlights the overwhelmingly important context in which we conduct the struggle for life and battle against the culture of death.

24. Quoted in Peterson, *Gray Dawn*, 247n19. James's novel provides an imaginative (and extreme) illustration of the moroseness that attends life in a world without children. The inescapable sense that the world is winding down and the effects this has on those remaining are well drawn, but zero or negative population growth do not quite mean a world without children. In contrast, though, Eberstadt ("Too Few People?" 55) has observed that as fertility in the modern world is falling, so too is childlessness. Although an increasing number of couples remain childless voluntarily, subreplacement fertility primarily means that almost everyone will have a first or second baby if they can, but very few will seek a third.

25. Gertrude Himmelfarb, "The Ghost of Parson Malthus," *Times Literary Supplement*, 23 January 1999.

26. Eberstadt, "Too Few People?" 55.

In Australia at least, few people, even Catholics, realize that no country in the Western world is producing enough children to maintain a stable population. Even fewer realize that if present trends continue depopulation consequences will be drastic for the Western world, representing a colossal shift (ultimately) in the balance of power. This is the other side of the coin: an unspoken motive for the First World enthusiasm to limit population in the Third World. Like the upper middle classes in nineteenth-century England, the rich Western countries do not want too many unruly poor, even at a distance! Our young people are well aware of the dangers of overpopulation, especially in Asia, and ignorant of what is happening at home. We too must not spend our time rearranging the deck chairs.

THE RELIGIOUS SITUATION IN AUSTRALIA

This background might be of some interest to those of other countries and provides the context for the three suggestions I will make.

I now want to spend a little time on the religious situation in Australia and the state of pro-life sentiment there. Many, or most, pro-life activists have come from the ranks of practicing Christians. Here our base is shrinking, and anti-life attitudes are influencing even churchgoers, and especially our young people. Christians are people of hope, champions of life for today and tomorrow, but none of us can choose the times in which we live and die. Apparently, a Chinese curse is that one should live in interesting times. We are on the brink of even more interesting times in the struggle for life, immersed in mighty forces of social, indeed global, change, which are largely beyond our control.

One of the most important of these forces is the (in the Western world at least) apparent waning of religious belief and commitment—as opposed to religious sentiment, which as the burgeoning of new-age cults and fads shows, is probably as strong as ever. In Australia, which has a population of a little over 20 million, the religious situation is within the parameters for the West, somewhere between the situations in the United States and the United Kingdom. The number of Australians who believe in God is large but falling, approximately 72 percent in the early 2000s, down from around 80 percent in the early 1990s.[27] In the U.S.A., by contrast, the figure is closer to 90 percent. While 82 percent of Americans are Christians,[28] the 2001 census put the total number of Christians in Australia at 68 percent, down from 74 percent in 1991.[29] As one might expect, not all of these regularly practice their religion in a formal way.

Catholic religious practice in particular, as measured by regular Mass attendance, has declined from about 55–60 percent in the 1950s and early 1960s[30] to 16 percent in 2001. Many "RCs" are not retired Catholics, but resting, relaxed, or reluctant Catholics. It is important to understand this practice rate comparatively. It means that in 2001 about 764,000 Catholics went to Mass each Sunday.[31] Among Australian Anglicans that year, who make up 21 percent of the population, only 178,000 worshiped each Sunday—an attendance rate of 4.5 percent. The exception for the Anglicans is the evangelical Sydney diocese, where attendance between 1996 and 2001 grew by 9 percent.[32] In every Catholic parish there is a hard core of dedicated believers, and it is these people who keep parish life alive.

27. Belief in God (meaning belief in either a personal god or some form of higher spirit or life force) was recorded by the Australian Community Survey (1998) and the Australian Wellbeing and Security Survey (2002) at 74 percent and 69 percent respectively. Given that belief in God is unlikely to have fallen by a six-point margin in four years, and allowing for the usual margin of error of 3 percent, both surveys are consistent with a result of 71 or 72 percent.

28. Baylor Religion Survey (Waco, TX: Baylor University, 2006).

29. Australian Bureau of Statistics, *Census, Australia 2001*.

30. Hans Mol, *Religion in Australia* (Melbourne: Nelson, 1971), 13–14. In 1954, according to Mol, Gallup Poll estimated that 75 percent of Catholics attended Mass weekly.

31. Australian Catholic Bishops Conference, Pastoral Projects Office, National Attendance Count 2001 (2002).

32. National Church Life Survey. Sydney: NCLS Research, 2001.

In the 2001 census Catholics constituted 26.7 percent of the Australian population, a percentage that has not varied much for forty years. Catholics replaced Anglicans as the largest denomination in 1986, and our numbers increased by 202,000 between 1996 and 2001, reflecting the steady increase in Australia's population. However, this increase, a percentage decline in 2001 of just over one-third of 1 percent for Catholics (in 1996 Catholics made up 27 percent of the population), masked a significant exodus, as Catholic migration should have pushed the percentage higher.[33]

The major difference between the religious situation in Australia and that in the United States is the weakness of Protestantism in Australia. Between the 1996 and 2001 censuses, many of the major non-Catholic but Christian denominations saw their number of affiliates decline, some by less than 1 percent (the Anglicans), some by almost 6 or 7 percent (the Presbyterian and Uniting churches respectively), while others recorded small growth (the Lutherans by 0.2 percent). Higher levels of growth were recorded by the Pentecostals (11.4 percent) and Baptists (4.8 percent), but although the percentage increase was significant the numbers involved were comparatively small.[34] As a percentage of the total population, most of the major denominations, including Catholics, have fallen by approximately 1 percent in the ten years between 1991 and 2001.[35] I do not rejoice in this at all. Unlike the United States, Australia has no real equivalent to the Southern Baptists, the Evangelicals, and therefore no Protestant basis for building something akin to Reagan's "moral majority," or even a powerful, organized, minority mass movement.

Another significant change between the 1996 and 2001 censuses was that the percentage of self-declared irreligious declined from 16.6 percent to 15.5 percent, the first such decline for one hun-

33. *Census, Australia 2001.*
34. Ibid.
35. Christian Research Association, *Australia's Religious Communities,* 2nd ed. (Melbourne: Christian Research Association, 2004).

dred years. This percentage still accounted for 2.9 million people, more than every Christian denomination except Catholics and Anglicans.[36] But there is no inevitable progression to majority secularism despite the political correctness and irreligion that dominate most of the media.

THE PRO-LIFE SITUATION IN AUSTRALIA

In 2004 there were approximately 90,000 abortions conducted in Australia, yielding a rate of 20.9 abortions per 1,000 women aged 15–44. This is one of the highest abortion rates in the developed world, with New Zealand, the U.S.A., and Sweden, and two and a half to three times the rate in the Netherlands and Germany.[37] It is estimated that approximately one-third of Australia women will have an abortion at some stage in their lifetime.[38] This means there is a huge emotional investment in these issues and often a grim determination not to hear the truth, especially from the Church. Abortion also seems to be one of those issues on which catechesis has varied in quality and effectiveness.

Meanwhile, the abortion industry is promoting a radical increase in the variety and quantity of abortion, at all stages of gestation. We are also amongst the world leaders in assisted reproductive technology, and therefore in embryo exploitation and destruction. The advent of cloning promises numerous further developments. Australia is also one of the few places in the world to have legally tolerated euthanasia at one time in one of its territories, and there is a continuing campaign to legalize it throughout Australia. But the overturning of the euthanasia legislation of the Northern Territory by the Federal Parliament, with the support of the prime minister and opposition leader, was a stunning victory.

36. *Census, Australia 2001.*
37. Statistics New Zealand, *Demographic Trends 2004* (2005).
38. Catherine Cotton and David Cotton, eds., *Abortion in Australia into the Twenty-First Century: Facts, Current Trends, and a Way Ahead* (Sydney: New South Wales Right to Life, 2006).

ATTITUDES OF AUSTRALIANS TO LIFE ISSUES

There are three constituencies everywhere in the struggle for life, present to different degrees in different countries and at different times: the minority of committed people who oppose us; the majority, who are often confused, sometimes hostile, sometimes indifferent, usually eclectic and at least partially open to persuasion; and the hard core of pro-life forces, preferably a coalition of people of all beliefs and no religious belief.

However, in Australia at least, it remains true that the strength of the pro-life forces comes from the Catholic community, where attitudes to moral questions are changing as moral uncertainty and confusion gather pace, especially among the young. To me, it is no coincidence that Holland, where Catholic faith and practice have collapsed so radically, is the euthanasia capital of the world. In Australia we have a lot of work to do to keep our home fires burning.

The vast majority of Australian church attenders think that human life is sacred and that access to abortion should be severely restricted. However, most church-attenders believe abortion is acceptable in the case of serious defect in the child, and a significant proportion think terminally ill people should be able to choose to die, whatever that means precisely. In general, practicing Pentecostals and Baptists tend to be much more anti-abortion and anti-euthanasia than Anglicans and members of the Uniting Church.[39]

In the 2001 National Church Life Survey many Catholic church-goers declared themselves at least partly at odds with Catholic teaching on abortion and euthanasia. Only 53.5 percent of Mass attenders said that they thought abortion is always wrong (up from 47 percent in 1996), and 36.2 percent said it is justified (only) in extreme circumstances (down from 42 percent in 1996). But there is a difference between people's private moral views and what they think the law should permit. This difference is particu-

---

39. National Church Life Survey 2001.

larly acute when it comes to abortion, and for Catholics too. Only
39.3 percent of Mass attenders said abortion should never be permitted. 45.4 percent said abortion should be permitted in extreme
circumstances, 4.9 percent said it should be available in a wider
range of situations, and 6.7 percent said it should be available on
demand. Almost 32 percent of Mass attenders agreed with voluntary euthanasia when it is requested by the terminally ill, with only
49.8 percent disagreeing (down from 51 percent in 1996).[40]

While there is some comfort in finding that the more frequently one attends Mass the more likely it is that one will oppose abortion and euthanasia, and in the more general finding that
Catholic and Evangelical church-attenders are still much more pro-
life than the general community, the churches clearly face an enormous pastoral task of preaching the Gospel of Life even to their
own members, and in offering people real alternatives to the culture of death and its supposed "solutions."

The capacity of a bishop to influence public opinion, as distinct from fostering the faith and moral beliefs of his community,
depends on many things, but especially on the size and wealth and
education of his own national faith community. A well-educated,
prosperous Catholic community of 30, 40, or 50 percent of the
population should be able to do more than a poor minority of 5
percent. Whether it will achieve more is another question!

We know grace builds on nature, and the religious decline in
so many places indicates not only that there is a weakness of faith,
but also that the traditional sociological forces of parish, school,
and family, supplemented by the activities of the religious orders,
are being overrun and are no longer adequate. We need new sociological agents, new sociological defenses, as well as interior faith
renewal. One part of this response is to use the secular media more
creatively.

40. Ibid.; National Church Life Survey 1996.

ABORTION RESEARCH

We all know that political parties do extensive polling to investigate public opinion—sometimes, it is claimed cynically, to devise policies that suit public opinion and enhance the chances of election or reelection, rather than responding to a situation with unpopular measures.

My suggestion is not simply to discover public opinion through short questions on the whole range of life issues (results that we know to be heavily influenced by the wording of the question), but to do extensive polling through long interviews with different representative individuals: young, old; male, female; Christian or neopagan; pro-life, pro-choice, or indifferent. Here we should be able to discover their individual points of view, why they hold them, and most importantly, what arguments they regard as persuasive, irrelevant, or counterproductive.

There is a legion of particular issues that might be explored.

Are logical arguments or anecdotes more effective, especially with the middle ground? In campaigning, how much of the message should be positive, how much negative?

In an age of individualism, how strong is the reluctance to judge another person? Are men particularly reluctant to impose their views on women? How pervasive is the conviction that mitigating circumstances can undermine any position of principle? Is the invocation of church authority a help or a hindrance? How influential is medical advice? Pro-life groups in Australia have traditionally emphasized the rights of the unborn child. Does this resonate with the general public, or do they see the issue almost exclusively as belonging to the woman involved? Does this mean that arguments should be focused more on how bad abortion is for the woman rather than on the killing of the aborted?

Is it useful or counterproductive for pro-life forces to emphasize the grief and guilt of the woman involved in abortion? Or would it be more effective with the middle ground we are attempting to convince, simply to acknowledge the intensely difficult situation of these mothers, building on the consensus that nearly everyone believes that fewer abortions would be better?

Does it help to compare abortions with the Holocaust? Does it help in opposing euthanasia to compare it with abortion? How frequently, if at all, should men or members of the Church hierarchy be used in campaigning against abortion? Is it effective with public opinion, or counterproductive, for bishops to address street rallies on life issues?

At a different level, how effective is the argument that a woman has a right to keep her baby, to resist pressures for abortion? How should we approach the important question of the father's role in deciding the fate of his child?

Are pro-life supporters as confident in expressing their views in public as the supporters of abortion and euthanasia? Do Christians recognize that their faith brings important moral consequences for daily living, including life issues, or is their faith compartmentalized, isolated from many of the difficult life decisions?

The answers to these questions are important for any strategy to influence public opinion. After discovering these answers, where do we start? One fascinating suggestion is to insert paid advertisements onto the evening radio frequencies listened to by young adults.

Some readers will be familiar with the article by Paul Swope that was published in *First Things* in 1998, outlining the strategy he uses for his work with the Caring Foundation in the United States.[41] It is woman-centered and designed to deter pregnant women from proceeding to an abortion, rather than influencing opinion more generally. His approach is also based on a series of in-depth, one-on-one interviews with people, the results of which he claims can be accepted at a better than 95 percent confidence level.

These studies help us understand the contradiction in many

41. Paul Swope, "Abortion: A Failure to Communicate," *First Things* 82 (April 1998) 31–35.

people's thinking who simultaneously believe that abortion is killing and also that it should be legally available. Swope points out that many young women have developed a sense of identity that emphasizes control and that does not include being a mother—at least not until other priority goals have been reached. "The sudden intrusion of motherhood is perceived as a complete loss of control over their present and future selves." The possibility of accepting an unplanned pregnancy is seen to mean the end of all their other aspirations—university, travel, career. If the pregnancy is accepted, then their life is "over," a feeling often reinforced by family, friends, and society at large. For a woman in such a crisis, there is felt to be no real choice. Abortion is a matter of survival.

Swope claims this is why the traditional approach emphasizing the humanity of the child in the womb and the evil of killing him has not made any decisive impression on opinion. It is seen by many as an unfeeling and judgmental response to women facing "death."

Swope suggests we need to reframe the debate to address the crisis of a woman with an unplanned pregnancy. She needs to be encouraged and reassured that going through with pregnancy will not mean the "end" of her life, and that she can regain control by actually deciding to accept the baby. TV advertisements developing these themes seem to have enjoyed some success, and although Swope's approach is regarded by some in the pro-life movement as controversial,[42] I think we need to look at it carefully if we are serious about making ground on abortion. It is not particularly useful to answer questions that people are not asking, even though a long-term strategy might be to encourage other questions.

Let me now conclude by mentioning three areas for foundational spiritual activity in the pro-life struggle, where a bishop might usefully be engaged.

---

42. See for example Scott Klusendorf, "The Vanishing Pro-Life Activist," *Christian Research Journal* 22:1 (Fall 1999): 23–25 and 42–45.

FAITH AND REASON

Pope John Paul II's 1998 encyclical, *Fides et ratio*, was addressed to bishops. Even today for some, and certainly for the Enlightenment thinkers of the past, it would seem strange that a pope, even a philosopher pope, should be urging Catholic bishops to defend reason.

This is now an important human as well as religious task for bishops because truth is under attack; indeed the very idea that there is truth at all is hotly disputed. This is reflected not merely in an explicit postmodernism, but even in Christian circles, where an incoherent relativism flourishes: "What is important is that you are comfortable with that"; "It depends on how each person feels." The Church is a partner with the rest of humanity in service of truth and should be a voice for truth.

This is not to suggest that the defense of truth is important because it is a useful moral, political, or therapeutic tool (although for our purposes in the struggle for life, it is certainly such). The systematic and intellectual search for truth develops from our sense of awe and wonder, which is rooted in our nature; such a search is also life enhancing. We are born to know, and it is one of humanity's greatest achievements (and a blessing) that we know so much. Knowledge as such is no threat or insult to God our Creator; rather it is a tribute to God, reflecting the development and use of gifts he has given us.

Pope John Paul spoke in this encyclical of faith and reason as "two wings on which the human spirit rises to the contemplation of truth."[43] However, they do not have the balanced function of a pair of wings, because reason has a certain primacy and cannot be judged by anything other than itself.[44]

While the heart still can have its reasons which reason does not know, all those interested in the struggle for life, as well as our

---

43. John Paul II, Encyclical Letter *Fides et ratio* (1998), preamble.
44. Hayden Ramsay, "The Philosophical Significance of *Fides et ratio*," *Philippiniana Sacra* 34:100 (January–April 1999): 79–91, at 79.

opponents who often stress adult autonomy, are interested in the reasons we adduce to support our claims. If the concept of truth, and especially moral truth, is removed from popular consciousness, the pro-life struggle becomes increasingly difficult and degenerates into a battle of personal preferences, even feelings.

PRIMACY OF CONSCIENCE

The English have an intriguing writer and intellectual, Felipe Fernández-Armesto, who writes extensively about the cultural hegemony of the United States, especially over small countries like Australia. He believes this culture of the United States is self-subverted by two genuine heresies, "the Lone Ranger heresy" and "the Donald Duck heresy."

The Lone Ranger is the successful man, who claims that he did it all by himself, the outsider who does not need society, who owes nothing to anyone. But my concern is with the consequences of the second heresy, the Donald Duck heresy, in the wider community, but especially among Catholics.

Donald Duck is warm-hearted and well disposed, believes in the natural goodness of man, and has an unshakeable conviction of self-righteousness. He means well and he is likable, despite his indulgence in all the vices of individualist excess: he knows it all; he is noisy and often bad-tempered at the incomprehension surrounding him. His activity is often disastrous, for himself and for others, but he means well. In the comic strips this is sufficient for all to be forgiven as we go to the next episode. But in real life this is a recipe for calamity.

Too many Donald Ducks produce the "feel good" society, which works to remove personal guilt, anything that would make people feel uncomfortable, so that complacent self-satisfaction becomes a virtue; confession is replaced by therapy and self-reproach by self-discovery.[45] Let me translate the Donald Duck heresy into

45. Fernández-Armesto, "America Can Still Save the World."

the terms of contemporary public debate on morality in Australia, where a goodly number of Catholics publicly espouse the primacy of conscience as a Catholic doctrine that has been long taught by the Church.

The primacy of conscience is of course one of the principal targets in Pope John Paul II's marvelous 1993 encyclical, *Veritatis splendor*. Only truth, or the Word of God, has primacy, is the ultimate rule of action, while individual conscience is a proximate norm, necessary but insufficient. Even a genuine searcher for truth can be mistaken, sometimes with disastrous consequences.

In *Veritatis splendor* John Paul II rejected certain currents of modern thought that absolutize freedom of conscience, so that it becomes the supreme tribunal of moral judgment, where the claims of truth are displaced by the criteria of sincerity, authenticity, and being at peace with oneself. He rejected this quasi-idolatry of freedom and sincerity.[46]

This primacy of conscience and rejection of moral truth, this repudiation of an objective moral order, is heavily influenced by secular intellectual currents; for example, relativism and the deconstructionists, as well as the imperatives of advertising in a consumer society. People often do not like being told what is right or wrong or what to do by authority figures, clerical or otherwise.

When Church leaders, clerical or lay, lapse into silence or are unable to argue convincingly for moral principles, even pro-life supporters who are pro-family and opposed to abortion and euthanasia can be tempted to see their position as an individual one, which they would not want to force onto others, especially by public legislation. This is no basis for action.

THEOLOGY OF THE BODY

In *Witness to Hope*, George Weigel claims that the theology of the body represents John Paul II's most important theological contri-

---

46. John Paul II, Encyclical Letter *Veritatis splendor* (1993), §§ 32; 35; 52; 54–64.

bution or development.[47] As archbishop of Krakow, Karol Wojtyła served on the committee established in the 1960s to reconsider the Church's teaching on artificial contraception. He was part of the minority whose advice was accepted by Pope Paul VI. Paul VI's reiteration of the traditional teaching on artificial contraception in 1968 after years of delay and rising expectations of change provoked a crisis of confidence like the Galileo case—one that has been compounded later by both pastoral and catechetical failure. Disagreement over this particular moral issue has played a major part in discrediting and casting doubt on the teaching capacity of the Church on moral matters, especially on sexuality. However, what is in dispute now within the Catholic community is not only natural family planning, but the whole range of Christian teachings on life and sexuality.

There is very little understanding in the public mind, even within the Catholic community, of the connection between the Pill as the trigger of a contraceptive mentality and the evil consequences for society that have followed. So a major task for the Church is to encourage people more and more to see the wisdom, both human and divine, of this particular teaching. John Paul II's theology of the body is a powerful aid to this purpose.

John Paul developed his theology of the body over four years at 130 papal audiences, beginning on 4 September 1979.[48] The central point is that human sexual love, within the sacrament of marriage, is an icon of the inner life of the Holy Trinity; that is, of God himself.

The cultural revolution of the 1960s and 70s saw the nature and limits of freedom hotly contested, especially in the area of sexuality. Modern mythology has it that the Pill freed women from the threat of pregnancy, although in fact it was not removed but radically reduced. The intolerance of limits in the sexual realm, often taken as a given today, is relentlessly reinforced by advertising, popular music, and films.

---

47. Weigel, *Witness to Hope*, 333–43.
48. John Paul II, *The Theology of the Body* (Boston: Pauline Books, 1997).

In this context it is increasingly difficult to get a hearing for Christian teaching on sexuality even among young Catholics, where incomprehension is a major reason for disaffection and lapsing from practice. The personal costs of sexual freedom and its illusory promises provide us with a unique long-term opportunity to offer healing, especially to those who have been wounded, and therefore to evangelize, initially with minorities, just as the Church grew in the Roman Empire. Church growth will follow only the faithful living and effective presentation of the fullness of Catholic teaching on life. No growth will follow from its dilution and deformation, or a tactful silence!

God created us male and female "from the beginning" (Mt 19:3–6). Our divine provenance imbues us with many wonderful privileges over other creatures. One is the human capacity to create "mirrors," to express and reflect God's creative power. Because we can think and choose freely we are also images of God.

It helps us to understand the nature of human sexuality if we reflect on Adam's original solitude. Neither the company of God nor that of the animals could console him. His loneliness was repaired only through the creation of Eve. Man and woman become images of God in the act of communion together, which requires a radical giving of the self and receiving of the other. We can see the oneness of man and woman in their original nakedness in the Garden, in the original solitude that brought the one to the other, and in the original unity that followed. The "bodyliness" of this unity is part of God's scheme, and it highlights that the body itself is not evil, despite tinea, piles, and dandruff.

Original sin disrupts the unity between man and God and between man and woman. Human flourishing depends on self-giving, not self-assertion, and this is particularly true in sexual love. Original sin compromises our capacity for self-giving, inclining us to treat the other as an object. It also introduces shame into the equation. Genesis is very clear that prior to eating from the tree of knowledge Adam and Eve were quite comfortable in their nakedness with each other. The intrusion of sin disrupted the unity between them and led them to see themselves no longer as one together, but as two separate creatures, who felt ashamed of their nakedness before each other and before God. This separation of the one into two automatically opens the possibility of treating and regarding the other as an object rather than as part of one's self.

In his catechesis on the theology of the body John Paul provoked considerable controversy with his warning against adultery of the heart. This was possible, he said, even within marriage when otherwise faithful spouses treat each other as objects in their sexual relations. The lines from Matthew's Gospel (Mt 5:27–28) where Our Lord warns against committing adultery in one's heart form a key reference for John Paul.

When love turns to lust male and female differences become a source of confrontation. The reality of sin makes the world a place of toil and fear and the human heart a battlefield between love and lust; self-mastery and self-assertion; freedom as giving and freedom as taking. Lust does not desire the good of the other. It uses the other as an object of pleasure. Christian ethics redeems sexuality from the trap of lust, just as purity of heart redeems the body.

Living the good life as created beings depends on living within the limits and according to the truths of the human condition. Purity of heart and the capacity to channel desires toward personal self-mastery in holiness are part of the high calling of the Christian life. These remain necessities, despite the promises of a false humanism that claims that human nature has neither limits nor boundaries, being infinitely plastic and malleable—a vain and counterproductive attempt to liberate humans from guilt.

Marriage is the most ancient sacrament. In the twelfth chapter of Mark's Gospel Jesus is asked who the widow of seven brothers will be married to in heaven. He replies that there is no marriage in heaven (Mk 12:18–26). This is not because we lose our bodies in heaven, but because there self-giving and reciprocity are perfect, first of all with God and then with others. There we undergo a divinization in some form to become like the risen Christ.

Celibacy in this context is an icon of heaven. It is lived in this life for the kingdom in anticipation of the heavenly state. It aspires to the perfect intersubjectivity that constitutes the final communion of saints. Lived well, it leads to a spiritual paternity and maternity.

This is also prefigured in the chasteness that marriage demands of spouses. Chastity, in the form of self-mastery, is essential to genuine self-giving. What does a man or a woman's "yes" mean if they are unable to say "no"? As self-giving, marriage is an icon of the union of God and his people, the Church. It is also an icon of the inner life of the Trinity. It reveals God's purposes in creation and redemption. Proper sexual love is an act of worship.

There is a painful ignorance among Catholic youth, and many older, on the rationale for the Christian teaching on life and sexuality. Often it is seen as an old-fashioned list of prohibitions, denying people their rights to sexual activity.

The theology of the body needs to be worked into our secondary school catechesis, showing that the essential linkage of the love between a man and woman, sexual intercourse and new life, is not only the best preparation for lifelong marriage and children, but also something sacred and important, reflecting the very life of the one true God.

CONCLUSION

In Australia at least, we might have understated the religious dimension in our argumentation in the struggle for life. Everywhere in the English-speaking world there is a majority of self-declared Christians; most of them and even the nonreligious, especially outside the circle of the opinion makers, are not truly secularized, but open in a muddled way to transcendence, superstitious and sentimental, as well as sometimes exercising genuine religious insight. Certainly they are moved more by their heartstrings than their head, often as open to religion and generalized Christian aspirations as they are to philosophical argumentation. I believe we do a disservice to God and probably to the pro-life cause if God is never mentioned in our pro-life arguments. But that might be another topic for another occasion, to be argued differently in different countries. It also goes without saying that prayer, conversion, and Christian living are mighty prerequisites for our struggle.

We need grace and hope, but we also need ideas and confidence and strategies for our struggle, not as an alternative to our basic Christian calling, but as an essential dimension of our response to Christ's gospel message.

8. THE CASE FOR GOD

GOD AND SCIENCE

Beginning in the second half of the eighteenth century science cast itself as the great antithesis of religion. For a while this looked rather convincing. What intelligent person could seriously prefer religion, with its superstitious beliefs in God, grace, the soul, and life after death, to science, with its clarity and light? From this point of view it was clearly desirable that science displace religion as the guiding force in people's lives, so as to put existence on a completely "rational" basis—which usually meant nothing more than placing it under the dominion of reductionist materialism.

Today science itself is divided on the meaning and implications of its discoveries. The British geneticist J. B. S. Haldane can be taken to speak for those who read science through the lenses of atheism. Once asked what he deduced about the nature of the Creator from his creation, Haldane replied: "An inordinate fondness for beetles."[1] The urbane derision of this remark marks a skepticism quite at odds with the attitudes of other eminent scientists who are at least able—in good scientific fashion—to keep an open mind on whether or not there is a God. Einstein said that with every advance, the physicist finds himself "astonished to notice how sublime order emerges from what appeared to be chaos."[2] This is not something the scientist reads into the universe; rather it reflects the inherent reality of the cosmos.

Who or what is God? This is a question that has exercised the minds of the best—and the worst—philosophers, scientists, and

---

The chapter was originally an address to the Faith and Reason Society of the University of New South Wales, Sydney, Australia, 5 October 2000.

1. Quoted in Bryan Appleyard, *Understanding the Present* (London: Picador, 1993), 107.

2. Quoted in ibid., 44.

theologians for millennia. One of the best, Professor Russell Stannard, summarized some of the issues involved in this question with his characteristic lucidity in a series of articles in 2000, published in the English Catholic magazine *The Tablet*.

Stannard rightly points out that God is not an object that exists, in the way we might speak of an apple existing. If this were all God was—an existent object—it would not shed much useful light on anything. Things have to be brought into existence, and to speak of God as an existent thing is only to raise the question who created God. Instead, we speak of God as the source of all existence, that which is responsible for the existence of things, the creator and sustainer of all that is. God is not the divine watchmaker of the deists, who sets everything going and then steps out of the picture. "He is involved at first hand in everything that goes on," not just a the first moment of creation.[3]

To ask "who created God?" is, strictly speaking, meaningless, because it confuses things that exist with the source of existence. Likewise, to try to think of God before space and time came into existence, before the Big Bang, is to make the mistake of assuming that God exists only in time. Certainly God can be found in time—every time we pray, in fact—but God is also beyond time. This is what we mean when we say God is eternal, although we are likely to become confused on this point if we make the mistake of thinking that eternity simply means limitless time, rather than the realm that transcends time.[4]

Being clear on these points is important for understanding the arguments made for God from the design of the universe. There are a weak and a strong version of this argument. The most probable basis of life is carbon, and for carbon to go through the processes that finally produce life, an immense span of time—which also means an immense expansion of the universe from the point of the Big Bang—would be required. In short, the universe has to be the size and age it is to support the existence of creatures such

3. Russell Stannard, "God and the Big Bang," *Tablet*, 22–29 April 2000.
4. Ibid.

as ourselves. This is known as the "weak anthropic principle," and it is reasonably uncontentious among scientists, although important nevertheless. It invites us to wonder about the way the universe has slotted itself together to produce beings who could wonder at it.[5]

This wondering leads to a stronger claim. Even if after the Big Bang a whole range of universes sprang up, covering every possible permutation of physical development, very few, and perhaps only our own, could attain "the alignment of qualities that would produce life." Our universe is the sort that produces things like us. "The fact of our existence must, therefore, condition the entire history of the universe." More than this, the production of human life must have been the goal our universe was heading toward from the beginning. This is known as the "strong anthropic principle" and its suggestion that the purpose of the universe is to produce life like ours is deeply contentious.[6]

There are two possible ways the universe came to exist: by chance or by design. All the evidence suggests that life and the physical structure of the universe had as much chance of being produced at random as the Mona Lisa had of being produced by a runaway truck moving through a rubbish tip. Stannard asks his readers to imagine that they had responsibility for designing a universe tailor-made for the development of life. Straight away they would face crucial questions such as how big the Big Bang should be. If the violence of this event is only a little less than needed, the gravitational pull of galaxies on each other would become so strong that they would be brought to a halt, and then brought back together to the collision point called the Big Crunch. All this would happen in a time shorter that the 12,000 million years needed for the evolution of human life.

If to avert this danger you erred on the other side, making the Big Bang slightly more violent than needed, other difficulties

5. Appleyard, *Understanding the Present*, 184–86.
6. Ibid., 186–87.

are encountered. The gases coming out of the Big Bang would be too fast to collect together and form embryo stars, meaning there would be no stars at all, and no life. As Stannard comments, "in fact it turns out that as far as the Big Bang violence is concerned, the window of opportunity is exceedingly narrow. If you are to get life in your universe, the thrust must be just right—as it happens to be with our actual universe."[7]

The same applies to the force of gravity. A little less than it actually is would produce no stars and no life, for although the Big Bang gases would collect together "to form dense clouds, the mutual gravity would not be strong enough to collect the amount needed to produce a temperature rise sufficient to light the nuclear fires." A little more gravity than needed would produce only the massive types of stars that burn themselves out too quickly. "For evolution to take place, you must have a steady source of energy for 5,000 million years," that is, a medium-size star like our sun.[8]

Then there are the materials from which you might like to build the bodies of living creatures. The hydrogen and helium released with the Big Bang are the two lightest gases, and to produce living bodies you need the nuclei of the heavier elements produced by the nuclear fusion in stars. This is not as easy as it might seem. Carbon is the decisive element, and the conditions for its emergence have to be just right. The odds against carbon being produced randomly are so great they led Fred Hoyle—the astrophysicist who first unraveled the mystery of carbon synthesis—to quip that "a common-sense interpretation of the facts suggests that a super-intellect has monkeyed with the physics."[9]

Hoyle offers another example of where this super-intellect has monkeyed with the physics. There are at least 100 billion galaxies like our own, twenty for every man, woman, and child in the world. There are at least 100 billion stars in our galaxy alone, and

7. Russell Stannard, "Traces of a Designer," *Tablet,* 6 May 2000.
8. Ibid., 606.
9. Ibid.

there are more stars in the universe than grains of sand on the earth. The number of subatomic particles in the entire universe has been calculated at 10^{81}. These are enormous numbers, beyond our comprehension. And yet the number that Hoyle and his collaborator Chandra Wickramasinghe came up with in the early 1980s when they calculated the odds of randomly shuffling amino acids to produce life is greater still: 10^{40000}.[10] To claim that life is a fluke against odds of this caliber is simply not tenable. It would seem, as Einstein once famously remarked, that "God does not play dice."[11]

The anthropic principles set out earlier find powerful support in these "coincidences." The universe seems to have bent over backward to accommodate us. As the physicist Freeman Dyson, winner of the prestigious Templeton Prize in 2000, has said, "the universe knew we were coming."[12] But if the universe does revolve around us after all, we still have to account for our puniness before the sheer expanse of the cosmos. The furthest galaxies are said to be 12 billion light years away, and light travels at 300,000 kilometers per second. How can we be of any importance before this inconceivable immensity?

But as the seventeenth-century French philosopher and mathematician Blaise Pascal once wrote: "Man is the feeblest reed in existence, but he is a thinking reed.... Though the universe were to destroy him, Man would be more noble than his destroyer, for he would know that he was dying, while the universe would know nothing of its own achievement."[13] Small and insignificant though we may appear to be, consciousness sets us apart from everything else in the universe. So far as we know at least, we are the only things that exist that have self-awareness, that can study the conditions we find ourselves in and offer an explanation of how the

10. "Darwin Wins," *Time*, 18 January 1982.
11. Quoted in Appleyard, *Understanding the Present*, 159.
12. Quoted in Stannard, "Traces of a Designer."
13. Quoted in Russell Stannard, "Who'd Swap with the Sun?" *Tablet*, 13 May 2000.

universe, with us in it, came to be. For nonbelievers, without human self-awareness there would be no truth, no goodness, and no beauty in the universe, and nothing to wonder at it.[14]

Could consciousness be the product of chance? For evolutionary scientists (and reductionists) such as Richard Dawkins, the answer is undoubtedly yes. From this perspective man is the product of processes that did not have him in mind. Evolution has produced in man a large brain, and "by some design fluke, a surplus of processing capacity emerge[d] which manifest[ed] itself as self-awareness." But this is a simply a claim that consciousness is a by-product of complexity. It explains nothing, least of all the experience of self-consciousness, the way we wonder about what something is, what it does, what it is there for, what it feels like, and what it means.[15]

A number of philosophers—most famously Daniel Dennett —have tried to give a complete account of conscious life in physicalist-functionalist terms. The inadequacies of this approach have been made clear by Professor John Haldane in two fine papers, "A Return to Form in Philosophy,"[16] and "The Diversity of Philosophy and the Unity of its Vocation."[17]

Evolutionists themselves emphasize that the evolution of human life is a highly improbable event, the result of a vast array of contingencies, each depending on prior contingencies: in short, flukes depending on flukes. We do not know enough about consciousness, or for that matter about the brain, to know whether the sort of incredible coincidences that go to making up the universe also apply here. But even if they do not, even if conscious-

14. For believers, human self-awareness is not necessary for the existence of these things at all. Even if we did not exist there would still be truth, goodness, and beauty, because these are transcendental properties, objectively existing and intelligently contemplated by nonhuman persons: that is, the angels.

15. Appleyard, *Understanding the Present*, 206–7.

16. In David Oderberg, ed., *Form and Matter: Themes in Contemporary Metaphysics* (Malden, MA: Blackwells, 1999).

17. In Anthony Fisher OP and Hayden Ramsay, eds., *Faith and Reason: Friends or Foes in the New Millennium?* (Adelaide: ATF Press, 2004).

ness really is the product of one fluke building on another, the possibility of design cannot be excluded. At the very least, given the improbabilities, the evolution of consciousness would seem to require something like divine guidance to ensure that the goal was reached. These and other limitations on evolutionary explanation have been very well set out by Professor Anthony O'Hear in his book *Beyond Evolution.*[18]

PHILOSOPHY AND GOD

Of course the notion of divine guidance is frequently misunderstood, by believers as well as nonbelievers. Pope John Paul II explained in *Fides et ratio* that the help philosophy can give us is incomplete and limited: living faith is required in order for us to know what we can of God. However, philosophical thinking can take us a certain way.

The most famous—and probably least understood—example of this is St. Thomas Aquinas's "Five Ways" of explaining God's existence, which appear as the second topic of his massive *Summa theologiae.*[19] The first topic, incidentally, is sacred study, demonstrating that reason does not replace revelation but complements it.

Pious tradition has it that Aquinas's first words were not "dada" or "mama" but "what is God?" These words remained on his lips until just before his death, when he finally acknowledged this question to be unanswerable: we cannot know *what* God is; however, philosophy can tell us *that* he is. This may not be enough to give us faith in God, but it can give us the confidence seriously to consider the faith.

Aquinas's Five Ways are often caricatured as "antique or Aristotelian science": we experience things that are moved; moving things need a mover; so ultimately, there must be a first or unmoved mover. This basic structure then seems to be reproduced

18. O'Hear, *Beyond Evolution.*
19. St. Thomas Aquinas, *Summa theologiae* (1–1, 2, 3).

in the other four "ways" dealing in turn with causation: possibility, perfection, and design in the world. But we should look more deeply at the structure of his argument.

If we ask what is really going on here, what we might discover is this: examining the world in any way—in five ways, or fifty, or five hundred ways—reveals that the world does not explain itself. Regarded not as a chain of moving things but rather as a system characterized by movement, the world raises the question "why is the cosmos as a whole the way it is—for example, why does it move?" Aquinas suggests the answer to this cannot be another part of the (moving) cosmos since that part would then itself require an answer. So, logically, the answer must be that which is not part of the cosmos. What is not part of the universe—what exists but is not a thing, an entity—is precisely, in Aquinas's words, "what men call God."

The deep structure of Aquinas's case for God, then, is this: the world does not explain itself; whether we focus on motion, causality, design, order, or any other aspect of our universe, we cannot account for that phenomenon without appealing to what is not part of the universe but is its source; that is, to God. Of course, Aquinas does not pretend his proofs are exhaustive, or that most people who believe in God come to faith through philosophical reflection. He accepts that people come to know that God exists by other ways than philosophical reflection. He certainly does not confuse intellectual assent to the existence of a god (in the manner of Australian scientist Paul Davies, for example)[20] with faith in the personal god of the monotheistic religions. But he does do a fine job of persuading us that philosophy takes us some distance to justifying God's existence and filling out a few of his attributes.

No Christian would be content with stopping the tale at our knowledge that God exists. Far more interesting is the question "What's he like?" We know very little about this. The Five Ways

20. Cf. Paul Davies, *The Mind of God: The Scientific Basis for a Rational World* (New York: Simon and Schuster, 1992), 194–222.

of arguing from the world to its Creator imply a little about him. But if we begin with the Creator himself, philosophy tells us much more about what he is not than what he is: God is *not* mortal, embodied, limited, or temporal. Is there anything a little more positive we can know of God's life? There is one overwhelmingly important fact. We can say that if God's life were to be projected onto human history as a film is projected onto a screen, it would take the form of the life of Jesus Christ of Nazareth. That is, at least for someone who accepts the Incarnation, Christ's life is God's inner life projected onto human history.

This is a strange idea. Christ's biography is one of suffering, rejection, and torture to death. Can it be true that this is God's life? Yes and no. Christ's life contains disaster not because he is God but because humanity is sinful. If pure love is projected onto human history, if God's Son is placed among sinners, he is kicked, shunned, and killed. The power of God's life is that from this mess he rises up, conquers death, and proclaims the reconciliation and healing of the world (including the reconciliation of all religions, as the Vatican document *Dominus Jesus* reaffirmed in 2000). God's life, then, is sheer love, and he reveals the power of love. Love will always be crucified and will always, powerfully yet lovingly, fight back.

The theological description of God's lovingness is "Holy Spirit," and that loving is focused on a concept or word (the eternal *Logos*), which Christians believe became the suffering and resurrected man of Nazareth. That is highly abstract. We need to recall also that God loves us personally. To understand this we need to ponder just what real love means. The word is diminished, if not trivialized, in our culture, but love is actually the most powerful part of our potential. If it is genuine, love will almost certainly involve suffering, but it will transcend the suffering, pointing it toward eternal life.

We should not forget that wherever we find ourselves, God found himself there too. In other words, we can talk to him about anything, with none of the embarrassment we might feel at speaking to parents, teachers, colleagues, or priests, because God loves us even in our darkest corners, corners he has investigated.

Thus we can know that God is, and knowing this, might feel encouraged to explore a little more what he is. This is a process that begins with speaking trustingly in prayer to the One for whom no one is unlovable.

SCIENCE AND PHILOSOPHY

Popular modern science has an ambivalent attitude toward the traditional idea of God as First Cause. Some of the so-called modern cosmologists, such as Paul Davies, have been happy to accept a contemporary version of this. We could put it this way: once we have something, it is possible to explain what it does and why (by Big Bang or some other theory); but why there is anything rather than nothing in the first place needs a radically different sort of explanation. There must be some cause that is not caused by any preceding cause but that always existed and that brings about the existence of the primitive universe.

Other scientific writers, for example Richard Dawkins, reject the First Cause altogether. He argues that the First Cause is quite unlike all other causes we know, so is incomprehensible to us, and therefore we should not believe in it. After all, believing in a First Cause is simply a factor of our peculiar evolutionary inheritance; and we—we being, one suspects, Oxbridge physicists and their graduates—have now evolved beyond this primitive stage and no longer need the supposition of a First Cause.[21]

There are two things worth saying here. The first is that it is true that the First Cause is unlike every other cause. That is why we call God the "Creator." The term indicates not one who puts things together to make new objects, like a joiner or technician, but one who brings about things where previously there was noth-

---

21. Cf. Alister McGrath, *Dawkins' God: Genes, Memes and the Meaning of Life* (Oxford: Blackwells, 2005), 57–60.

ing. God's causality, we say, is ex nihilo—from nothing. Dawkins is right that this sort of causality is incomprehensible to us. But there are two types of incomprehensibility. Some things are incomprehensible because of our limitations. Other things are incomprehensible because by their nature they exceed human comprehension. This latter incomprehensibility is what Christians mean when they refer to God's causality as "essentially mysterious." It is not that our minds are too weak to grasp it but that it is not graspable by any mind, however strong. It is quite rational to believe in something essentially mysterious if there are good grounds for doing so. Indeed, anyone with a spiritual sense of any sort will do just that.

The second point about the First Cause is a point about existence. The existence of any thing depends on something else. A chair need not have existed, and does so only because of the efforts of other things and people which brought it about. These other things too were caused to exist by yet other things, and so on. But if the series of causes that explains a chair's existing never came to an end, then we would never actually have an explanation of the chair's existing; all we would have is an indefinitely, and infinitely, postponed promise of an explanation. Thus the explanation of the existence even of a simple chair implies there is, ultimately, a cause that is not itself in need of a further cause. In other words, there must be something whose existence needs no further explanation, or to put it another way, something that cannot be conceived of as not existing—something whose very nature or essence includes existence. This is what monotheistic faith refers to as "God."

So God is a cause, and in a quite different way from other causes, because he does not explain how changes come about but why there are things to change in the first place. Thus the thesis of God the Creator is fully compatible with any good scientific hypothesis about the events that launched the universe as we know it. As Catholic tradition affirms, theology is consistent with all good science. All truths form a unity.

THE ADVANTAGES OF BELIEF

Aside from the very good—and in some cases quite powerful—arguments for God from science, there is the lived experience of believers and the benefits that regular prayer and religious practice bring to everyday life. Strictly speaking, of course, just because the way of life believers adopt is beneficial in certain respects does not mean that there is a God. But it is worth something to demonstrate that lived religion can be positive, and regularly makes a contribution to the good life of many people.

I should also acknowledge that there is a slight chance of scandal in the spectacle of a Catholic bishop arguing for God and encouraging people to believe with an appeal to self-interest. However, the Lord himself encouraged those with heavy burdens to come to him for refreshment.[22] Certainly if this was the best we could do—and especially if it was the best a bishop could do—it would be insufficient. But given that we have good grounds both from the evidence of the physical world and from the world of reason and philosophy for believing in God, I do not think it hurts to tell people that in addition to all these good reasons, faith works. Being a believer brings real long-term advantages and generally helps to make our lives happier and more peaceful. Many more people come to believe through the service or heroic witness of Christians than through academic argumentation.

To begin with, faith in God gives meaning and purpose to our lives. The modern world is, for most in Australia certainly, a healthier, more comfortable, and more peaceful and stable place to live in than any our ancestors in human history knew. Nevertheless, illness and physical suffering continue to be an inescapable part of life. We prize our individualism highly, and the decline of tight-knit community and the loosening of bonds even within the family have produced new forms of suffering that most of us encounter at some point in our lives. Loneliness, uselessness, despair,

22. Mt 11:28.

and a powerful sense of the absurdity of it all are more prevalent than often acknowledged, and anxiety, it is probably fair to say, is at epidemic proportions. Rising suicide rates among young men[23] and the levels of drug abuse in Western societies give only a partial indication of the problem, because they register only those whose turmoil has reached the extreme. The comfort and serenity that regular prayer can bring to us in our suffering is real, and the need for it today in the absence of the old communal and social supports is greater than ever before. The same can be said of God's forgiveness, the need for which has not diminished in any way.

There are other benefits as well. Since the late 1990s a number of studies have been published suggesting that regular religious practice improves health and prolongs life. The health benefits are said to include lower blood pressure, smaller chance of stroke, and significantly reduced danger of dying from diabetes or respiratory and infectious diseases.[24] In one study from 1999, researchers in the United States found a seven-year difference in life expectancy between those who never attended religious services and those who attended more than once a week,[25] and a "meta-analysis" conducted in 2000 found a small but solid association between increased

23. In the period 1921–25 in Australia, the suicide rate (number of suicides per 100,000 persons) for men aged 15–24 years was 8.6. In the period 1996–98 it was 27.7. Similarly for the 25–34 age group, the rate rose from 19.9 to 37.0. The rate for women aged 15–24 years doubled in this time (from 3.0 to 5.9), but has remained steady for other age groups. One of the interesting questions the figures highlight is that while suicide rates for young men have risen, those for middle-aged and old men have fallen significantly, in some cases by more than half. See Australian Bureau of Statistics, *Suicides, Australia 1921–1998*. Since 1997 total suicide rates have fallen from 14.7 to 10.4 in 2004. But suicide remains a major external cause of death, with the total number between 1994 and 2004 outnumbering the total number of deaths from transport accidents over the same period. See Australian Bureau of Statistics, *Suicides, Australia 1994–2004*.

24. See for example D. Oman and D. Reed, "Religion and Mortality among the Community-Dwelling Elderly," *American Journal of Public Health* 88:10 (October 1998): 1469–75; and H. G. Koenig, et al., "Does Religious Attendance Prolong Survival?" *Journals of Gerontology. Series A, Biological Sciences and Medical Sciences* 54:7 (July 1999): M370–M376.

25. Robert A. Hummer, et al., "Religious Involvement and US Adult Mortality," *Demography* 36:2 (May 1999): 273–85.

life expectancy and weekly religious observance.[26] These are contentious claims, and the evidence for them is disputed in some cases.[27]
Apart from the inherent difficulties of demonstrating an association between faith and good health to scientific standards, attempts
to do so need to deploy highly technical forms of statistical analysis, which means that only specialists can judge whether such associations are correctly drawn.[28] But the very fact that medical scientists are paying serious attention to the possibility of a link between
good health and faith is itself an interesting phenomenon.

Various explanations are offered for these results. Researchers
point to the fact that people who practice their faith are more likely to have a supportive network of people around them who can
help in times of anxiety and trouble. Religious people generally
avoid behaviors that expose others to sickness and disease—for example, heavy drinking and smoking, drug taking, and promiscuous
sex. Some commentators attribute better health to a stronger im-
mune system, produced by the positive mental images and reduced
stress that regular prayer brings.

What of the effect of praying for someone who is sick? In a
1999 study, half the patients in a coronary care unit in an American hospital were randomly selected for intercessionary prayer by
a Christian prayer group. The intercessors were only told the first
names of their patients and prayed for them four times a day. The
patients themselves did not know they were being prayed for. Tak-

26. Michael E. McCullough, et al., "Religious Involvement and Mortality: A
Meta-Analytic Review," *Health Psychology* 19:3 (May 2000): 211–22.

27. For an important contribution skeptical of the many studies claiming a
link religious practice on good health, see R. P. Sloan, E. Bagiella, and T. Powell,
"Religion, Spirituality and Medicine," *Lancet* 353:9153 (20 February 1999): 664–67.

28. For an example of how technical this analysis can be, see Daniel E. Hall,
"Religious Attendance: More Cost-Effective than Lipitor?" *Journal of the American
Board of Family Medicine* 19:2 (March 2006): 103–9. Hall concludes that while the data
available for research in this area are limited, "the practical, real world significance
of regular religious attendance (2 to 3 additional life years) is similar to widely
recommended health practices like physical exercise....... Rather than dismissing
this finding as weak or non-existent, it may be more fruitful to invest the necessary
resources to better understand the nature and relevance of the association between
religious attendance and health."

en over a group of 990 patients, the study found that those who had been prayed for enjoyed a significantly lower rate of relapse after discharge.[29] I remain skeptical about such studies. In my experience the effects of prayer are usually less obvious and direct. A systematic review of the studies on the effects of intercessory prayer conducted first in 1998 and then substantively reviewed in 2000 concluded that there are no grounds at present for medical practitioners to change current practices, but the evidence so far gathered "is interesting enough to justify further study."[30]

On the broader question of the relationship between faith and good health, 1,200 studies and 400 reviews were critically analyzed in the *Handbook of Religion and Health* (2001),[31] concluding (as the *British Journal of Medicine* explained in a favorable editorial at the end of 2002) that a 60–80 percent "relation between better health and religion or spirituality is found in both corelational and longitudinal studies" covering a wide range of major health problems.[32] Some discussion has also focused on whether the benefits claimed for religious belief are related to the greater religiosity of the American population, and whether similar results would apply to a less religious population such as that of Australia.[33]

29. William S. Harris and Manohar Gowda, "A Randomized, Controlled Trial of the Effects of Remote Intercessory Prayer on Outcomes in Patients Admitted to the Coronary Care Unit," *Archives of Internal Medicine* 159:19 (25 October 1999): 2273–78. See also the discussion about this study in *Archives of Internal Medicine* 160:12 (26 June 2000): 1875–78.

30. L. Roberts, I. Ahmed, and S. Hall, "Intercessory Prayer for the Alleviation of Ill Health," *Cochrane Database of Systematic Reviews* 2000, Issue 2. Art. No.: CD000368. The same year, the *New England Journal of Medicine* also published an opinion article that argued strongly that whatever the effects of religion on health, medical practitioners should refrain from incorporating it into their practice for various reasons. See R. P. Sloan, et al., "Should Physicians Prescribe Religious Activities?" *New England Journal of Medicine* 342:25 (22 June 2000): 1913–16. Although some of the literature on this question was referred to in the article, no serious review of it was attempted.

31. Harold K. Koenig, Michael E. McCullough and David B. Larson, *Handbook of Religion and Health* (Oxford: Oxford University Press, 2001).

32. Larry Culliford, "Spirituality and Clinical Care," *British Journal of Medicine* 325 (21–28 December 2002): 1434–35.

33. See the exchange between Hedley G. Peach, "Religion, Spirituality and Health: How Should Australia's Medical Professionals Respond?" *Medical Journal of*

Religion also brings benefits for marriage and family life. Based on past patterns in Australia, 32 percent of future marriages are likely to end in divorce. In 2003, the divorce rate (per 1,000 married persons) was 13.1, up from around 10.7 in 1989.[34] In contrast, the 2001 National Church Life Survey, which surveyed over 78,000 Mass-goers, indicated that a little under 6 percent of those who attend Mass regularly or semi-regularly were divorced.[35] This figure for practicing Catholics—as opposed to census Catholics who almost parallel the trends of society as a whole—does not surprise me at all. A couple that regularly prays and worships together has a great source of strength and guidance available to them, especially in times of strain. However, we do not know how many regularly practicing Catholics cease practicing after divorce because of the Church's teaching against it.

Contrary to some expectations, cohabitation is not a good preparation for marriage. A study made in the late 1990s in Australia showed that after five years of marriage 13 percent of those who cohabited are likely to divorce, compared to 6 percent of those who had not cohabited. At the fifteen-year mark the proportions are 26 percent and 14 percent respectively, and at the twenty-five year mark they are 56 percent and 27 percent.[36] These Australian figures have been corroborated by similar studies overseas, although

Australia 178:2 (20 January 2003): 86–88; and Harold G. Koenig, "Religion, Spirituality and Health: An American Physician's Response," ibid., 51–52.

34. Australian Bureau of Statistics, _Divorces, Australia 2003._

35. National Church Life Survey. This figure includes 2.8 percent of respondents who indicated that they were remarried after divorce. The survey did not include questions about annulment and remarriage.

36. Australian Bureau of Statistics, _Marriages and Divorces, Australia 1999._ In another study, sociologists at the University of Queensland found that premarital cohabitation, as well as premarital childbearing, significantly increase the odds of marital breakup. While cohabitation increases the odds of divorce by 41 percent for men and 31 percent for women, out-of-wedlock childbearing increases those same odds by 63 percent for men and by 2.3 times for women. On the other hand, the birth of a first child within marriage had just the reverse effect, reducing the odds of marriage breakdown by 85 percent. See Belinda Hewitt, Janeen Baxter, and Mark Western, "Marriage Breakdown in Australia: The Social Correlates of Separation and Divorce," _Journal of Sociology_ 41 (June 2005): 163–83.

there have also been some findings suggesting that the link between premarital cohabitation and reduced chances of a marriage surviving may be diminishing, or even become statistically insignificant.[37] More generally, cohabitation is four or five times more unstable than marriage, and possibly as much as ten times more unstable where very young children are involved.[38]

The traditional Christian teaching on sexuality and marriage prohibits cohabitation, of course, although even believers tend to presume that young Catholics "shack up" pretty much at the same rate as nonbelievers. But a 1999 study showed that 48 percent of those who were married in a Catholic ceremony were cohabiting, compared to 69 percent for all couples marrying that year.[39] My private secretary was impressed by these figures, but he is of a different and younger generation. To me it remains disappointing and scandalous, but we should be grateful for the small mercy that we have not yet caught up with the rest of the population! On the evidence just discussed, the lower rate of cohabitation among Catholics is certainly a help in making their marriages work and significantly reduces the likelihood of divorce.

The teachings of the Church in this and other areas are not always easy, but making a sincere effort to follow them does help in leading happier lives. Morality is not a series of hurdles in an obstacle race but a powerful and effective guide to human well-being. This has important social implications too. We all have an interest in establishing strong healthy families, for the sake of the couples

37. David de Vaus, Lixia Qu, and Ruth Weston, "Premarital Cohabitation and Subsequent Marital Stability," *Family Matters* 65 (Winter 2003): 34–39.

38. Barry Maley, *Family and Marriage in Australia* (St. Leonards: Centre for Independent Studies, 2001), 27. See also Patricia Morgan, *Marriage Lite* (London: Institute for the Study of Civil Society, 2000), 20–22. Morgan refers to findings cited in the 1998 Report of the Australian House of Representatives Standing Committee on Legal and Constitutional Affairs inquiry into aspects of family services ("the Andrews Report"), which showed that cohabiting couples are almost ten times more likely to break up 18 months after the birth of a child than married couples. At the eighteen-month mark, 19 percent of cohabiting couples have broken up, compared to 2 percent of married couples.

39. *Marriages and Divorces, Australia 1999.*

involved and for their children. It is not just individual well-being that religion contributes to here. It also helps ensure that we remain a prosperous, peaceful, and decent society.

A simple, everyday example of this is volunteering. Thirty-two percent of the Australian population engaged in some form of voluntary work during 2000 (excluding the Sydney Olympics), up from 24 percent in 1995. Volunteering was highest (at 40 percent) among people aged 35 to 44, who are also those most likely to have young children or family commitments.[40] This provides an interesting contrast to the findings of another study, which found that many of the countries with low birth rates also rank at the lower end of the scale for volunteering, perhaps underscoring the way having children around makes us both more hopeful and less selfish.[41]

Volunteering among young people also increased considerably between 1995 and 2000, with 15 percent of 13–29-year-olds ("Generation Y") contributing five hours or less a month of volunteer work or community service, and another 12 percent contributing more than five hours monthly. Interestingly, Catholic or Anglican Gen Ys were not as strongly represented in higher levels (more than five hours per month) of volunteering as other Christian Gen Ys and those with no religious identification. However, at the lower levels of volunteering (five hours or less per month) there were more Catholics and more Anglicans involved when compared with those with no religion. In total 28 percent of Gen Y Catholics were volunteers, 24 percent of Gen Y Anglicans, and 23 percent of Gen Ys with no religion.[42]

The contribution made by volunteers is considerable. In Australia in 1995 volunteers donated almost 512 million hours of voluntary work. By 2000 this figure (again, excluding the impact of the Sydney Olympics) had risen to 704 million hours (although

40. Australian Bureau of Statistics, *Australian Social Trends 2002.*
41. *Australian Social Monitor* 3:1 (July 2000).
42. Michael Mason, et al., "The Spirit of Generation Y: The Final Report of a Three Year Study," unpublished report to project sponsors, 2006, chapter 6.

the average hours per volunteer remained the same, at 3.1 hours per week).[43] Not surprisingly, churchgoers are more likely than any other group to be involved in voluntary work, and volunteerism increases in direct proportion to a person's level of church attendance, with 57 percent of those attending church weekly volunteering, compared to 37 percent of those who attend only for the great Christian festivals, and 30 percent of those who only go to church once a year. Only 23 percent of those who never darken the door of a church volunteer.[44]

CONCLUSION

In the early nineteenth century the militant secularism that arose from the Enlightenment and the French Revolution confidently predicted a "withering away of religion" as the life of man was increasingly placed on a "scientific" footing. If one thing is clear to us as we commence the third Christian millennium it is that this great conceit has been utterly discredited. The failure of the secularization thesis has been spectacular, and not only in the Western nations, where it was first expected to be confirmed. Not only does the need for faith continue to haunt the spirit of man, but the complexities of modern life and the fragmentation of values in modern societies have made this need stronger than ever before.

Far from discrediting religion, science provides new grounds and reasons for the existence of God. In the area of philosophy the genuinely interesting and exciting developments are in the areas of natural law and the philosophy of religion. The old liberal-utilitarian project in philosophy, while still very strong, is increasingly bereft of new ideas and has not been able to free itself from its inherited nineteenth-century presuppositions. And at the practical everyday level it is becoming increasingly clear that religion is

43. *Australian Social Trends 2002.*
44. *Australian Social Monitor* 3:1 (July 2000).

useful—probably essential—for the strength and health of society's institutions and civic life.

It is no longer the case for God that is difficult to make. More and more it is the rational case *against* God that appears incoherent and in need of explanation. None of which means the task of evangelization has become any easier. But it is a help to be working intellectually with the wind behind us. Despite very real obstacles and challenges, these are important signs of hope. We should take our courage from them as we continue heading into other contrary winds.

9. THEOLOGY AND THE UNIVERSITY

Newman was a university man and knew the university well, not just as a Fellow of Oriel College but also as vicar of St. Mary's church in Oxford. He was renowned as a university preacher, with Gladstone describing him as the most powerful influence with students since Abelard.[1]

The Second Discourse in Newman's *The Idea of a University* (the original lectures were delivered in 1852) makes very clear his conviction that theology is not just mystification and metaphysics, but hard knowledge. Newman preferred to speak of the *circle* (rather than *hierarchy*) of knowledge as a way of emphasizing the interdependence of its various branches. But theology was the principal science in this circle, the first among equals, because "it comes from heaven ... its truths were given once for all at the first ... they are more certain on account of the Giver than those of mathematics."[2]

It is an indication of the nature of much contemporary theological discussion that this frank statement of faith in the decisive quality of revelation would be greeted by many with embarrassment. But Christianity has never considered itself as only a form of religious myth, sometimes competing with other offerings. In the classical world myth and religion were treated as matters of poetry and presentiment. They served an important function in justi-

---

This chapter was originally an address to mark the bicentenary of Newman's birth, Newman College, University of Melbourne, Melbourne, Australia, 17 February 2001.

1. David Newsome, *The Convert Cardinals: John Henry Newman and Henry Edward Manning* (London: John Murray 1995), 103.

2. John Henry Newman, *The Idea of a University* (1873), ed. Ian Ker (Oxford: Clarendon Press, 1976), 54 & 57–58. See also Ian Ker, *John Henry Newman: A Biography* (Oxford: Clarendon Press, 1988), 392.

fying political and social arrangements—as today they are said to perform an important therapeutic function—but did not belong to the order of reality as such. Christianity, however, based itself from the beginning not on myth but on philosophical rationality. It was not content to rely on a social, political, or therapeutic justification and to worship in the absence of truth, but appealed to knowledge and to the rational analysis of reality. Christianity displaced myth "not by virtue of a type of religious imperialism but as the truth which renders the apparent superfluous."[3]

Newman would not have expressed the matter quite in this way, but this basic historical fact underlies his conviction that religion and knowledge are not opposed to each other but indivisibly connected. For this reason, "Knowledge and Reason are sure ministers to Faith."[4] "The Church fears no knowledge," although secularized knowledge often fears the Church. This is not because the Church's claims are intrinsically ridiculous or unreasonable but because they emphasize truths about given questions (the humanity of the unborn child, the humanity of the old, disabled, and sick, the wrongness of unjust working conditions) that many in our society would prefer to disregard for a wide range of reasons. Knowledge that radically excludes the transcendent dimension of life is knowledge that has partly blinded itself. The diminishment of knowledge without faith is one reason why Newman insisted that although the value of knowledge is absolute, knowledge itself is "emphatically not the highest good." In Newman's view "it is better to have a simple faith than an educated intellect without religious belief."[5]

Newman is undoubtedly an admirer and defender of a liberal education, but he qualifies his support for this goal by systematically reminding his readers of its limitations. "Newman is keenly

---

3. Joseph Ratzinger, "Christianity: The Victory of Intelligence over the World of Religions," *30 Days* 1 (2000): 33–44, at 35–36.

4. Newman, *The Idea of a University*, ed. Ker, 6 and 198; Ker, *John Henry Newman*, 384.

5. Ker, *John Henry Newman*, 384.

aware of the danger of exaggerating the importance both of the university and of a liberal education. It is, he insists, 'as real a mistake to burden' liberal knowledge 'with virtue or religion as with the mechanical arts'":

> Its direct business is not to steel the soul against temptation or to console it in affliction, any more than to set the loom in motion, or to direct the steam carriage . . . it as little mends our hearts as it improves our temporal circumstances. . . . Quarry the granite rock with razors, or moor the vessels with a thread of silk; then you may hope with such keen and delicate instruments as human knowledge and human reason to contend against those giants, the passion and pride of man.[6]

Education is a great thing and should be appreciated for what it is. It is vain to make it the sole basis of happiness, virtue, or faith. These things require a more hardy foundation. Once that foundation is laid, however, education can be a powerful aid to making them flourish, and to deepening our appreciation of what they entail.

It is not only faith that needs a hardy foundation to make the most of education. Education also needs faith if it is to avoid "the tendency of the intellectual culture" to become "a false philosophy" and "a spurious religion." Newman gives the example of Constantine's nephew, Flavius Claudius Julianus (332–63), who is still known to us today as Julian the Apostate. Julian was superbly educated in Neo-Platonism and in the Athenian schools. St. Gregory of Nazianzus was a contemporary there, but while at Athens Julian was initiated into the Eleusinian mysteries. Once he became emperor in 361 he determined to degrade Christianity and promote paganism by every means short of open persecution—much like the approach of the neo-pagans today. One important element of this was encouraging internal dissension in the Church. To all of this was added the conspicuous example of Julian's personal austerity and strong sense of purpose. He appeared to be the model of philosophical virtue, although "every Catholic sees [in him]

6. Ibid., 385; & Newman, *The Idea of a University*, ed. Ker, 110–11.

the shadow of the Antichrist."[7] Ultimately, however, his attempts to revive paganism failed because of the shallowness of his particular philosophical religion and his failure to develop a cogent and coherent pagan theology. Education without faith—or in Julian's case, education against faith—is not sufficient to prevail in the long run, and this may be one of the reasons why our society and our universities have come to excel at producing people whose technical capacities are finely developed, but out of all proportion to the development of their capacity for dealing with—or even being alive to—the ethical dimensions of their work and the broader impact of religious questions upon their lives.

However, "we should not be misled by the dramatic vividness with which Newman depicts the effects of religionless culture into imagining a conflict that is not there." He makes a crucial distinction between "the *religion of* intellectual culture and religion itself." In practice "intellectual culture has also in moral matters 'a special claim upon our consideration and gratitude.'" The "religion of Civilization" is not incompatible with "the profession of Catholicism." Where there is conflict it is more important and fundamental, for it concerns the admissibility of theology as "a genuine branch and religion as a genuine part of the subject matter of knowledge." At a subsidiary level it is also over Catholicism taken "chiefly as a system of pastoral instruction and moral duty" and its bearing on those "subjects to which the cultivated intellect will practically be turned."[8] The exclusion of theology and religion from these questions and from knowledge itself is not demanded by any of the sciences. "No science can actually be hostile to theology," Newman argues. If any field of knowledge is hostile to theology and religion it is because it has been "infected" by a particular "Private Judgment" to that effect.[9]

Newman traces the view that religion is a matter of "feeling

7. Ker, *John Henry Newman*, 386.

8. Newman, *The Idea of a University*, ed. Ker, 158–59 and 162; Ker, *John Henry Newman*, 388.

9. Ker, *John Henry Newman*, 396; Newman, *The Idea of a University*, ed. Ker, 92.

or sentiment" rather than knowledge to the Reformation: "As the Lutheran leaven spread, it became fashionable to say that Faith was not an acceptance of revealed doctrine, not an act of the intellect, but a feeling, an emotion, an affection, an appetency; and, as this view of Faith obtained, so was the connexion of Faith and Truth and Knowledge more and more either forgotten or denied." Religion is still seen today as something that meets certain human needs and not as "an external fact and a work of God." It is useful in many ways, and perhaps ineradicable because of the needs it meets, but its basis is not reason. Habit, prejudice, loyalty, feudalism, "enlightened expedience"—any of these could be used as a basis for religion, but not reason and knowledge.[10]

This view of religion as a social construct ignores the central fact that religion's main purpose is knowledge: knowledge of God. For the great monotheistic religions, God is (as Newman describes him):

an Individual, Self-dependent, All-perfect, Unchangeable Being; intelligent, living, personal, and present; almighty and all-seeing, all remembering; . . . who will judge every one of us, sooner or later, according to that Law of right and wrong which He has written on our hearts . . . [who has] implicated himself in all the history of creation, the constitution of nature, the course of the world, the origin of society, the fortunes of nations, the action of the human mind; and who thereby necessarily becomes the subject matter of a science, far wider and more noble than any of those which are included in the circle of secular Education.[11]

A university, by its very name, professes to teach universal knowledge. Newman appreciates very well that if a university teaches nothing about "the Supreme Being" it is because it holds "that nothing is known for certain about the Supreme Being; nothing such as to have any claim to be regarded as a material addition to the stock of general knowledge existing in the world." But both from reason and revelation, Newman argues, "something very con-

10. John Henry Newman, *The Idea of a University*, ed. Martin J. Svaglic (South Bend, IN: University of Notre Dame Press, 1982), 21–22.
11. Ibid., 27.

siderable is known about the Supreme Being," and it make the university's claim to knowledge absurd if the "foremost" field of knowledge is excluded from it.[12]

Knowledge, not the domination of "private views" or ideology, should be the purpose of the university—fond hope it is—and because knowledge rather than the supremacy of a particular or private worldview is the goal, those who make up a university community have no need to "shrink from the co-operation of those who hold opposite views."[13] A university does not need to be a religious community, and even in a Catholic university not its all members need to be religious themselves, although the leadership cohort and considerably more than a majority of the staff should be. What is crucial, however, is a commitment to knowledge over opinion, and an acceptance that theology and religion are matters of knowledge, not therapy.

As knowledge, the goal of theology is "a true apprehension of God." "Nothing is easier than to use the word [God], and mean nothing by it." Today as in the pre-Christian past, people will say "'God wills' when they mean 'Fate'; 'God provides' when they mean 'Chance'; 'God acts' when they mean 'Instinct' or 'Sense'; and 'God is everywhere' when they mean 'the Soul of Nature.'" Part of the great appeal of the New Age movement is that allows one to give the word *God* whatever meaning is useful or consoling for one's immediate purpose. This sort of thing, as we know, has also infected theology. Using God in this way, that is in any way we like, undermines the justification for including theology and religion in the university, because it removes them from the realm of knowledge to the realm of personal preference and purpose. God is "something infinitely different from a principle, or a center of action, or a quality, or a generalization of phenomena."[14] God is not just something vague, or even very specific, about nature, in the broadest sense of that word. He is more than nature. This is the reason

12. Ibid., 18.   13. Ibid.
14. Ibid., 28.

why religion belongs to knowledge, and why theology, in New-man's view, is the foremost among the sciences.[15]

Truth, still, relies on metaphysics. This is despite the best efforts of secular philosophy over the last two hundred years. Nietzsche understood very well that objective truth and an objective sense of right and wrong relies on metaphysics, on knowledge of a realm beyond nature.[16] One of his many contemporary disciples, Richard Rorty, is tireless in proselytizing Nietzsche's claim that we must "overcome" metaphysics and stop thinking that knowledge, truth, and right and wrong require a foundation beyond the contingencies of human life.[17] On one thing, however, Newman, Nietzsche, and Rorty agree: metaphysics can be dispensed with only if we can finally dispense with the concept of absolute truth.[18] Until that day arrives, theology as "the science of God, or the truths we know about God put into a system," will continue to form part of knowledge, for he is "the invisible, intelligent Being" behind "the veil of the visible universe," acting on and through it, and distinct from it;[19] the guarantor of truth and justice, and the reason why, in the end, knowledge forms a unity rather than a rubbish bin of discrete and hopelessly fragmented disciplines.[20]

It was this central problem that Pope John Paul II addressed in his landmark 1998 encyclical *Fides et ratio*. The central claim advanced there is the inseparability of theology and philosophy. To understand our faith—to theologize in the Catholic tradition—we need philosophy. We must use the philosophical language of God, person, creation, relationship, identity, natural law, virtues, conscience, moral norms if we are to think about religion and de-

---

15. Ibid., 31.

16. Nietzsche, *The Gay Science*, 200–201.

17. Rorty, *Contingency, Irony and Solidarity*, chapters 1–3.

18. Newman, *The Idea of a University*, ed. Svaglic, 39: "I supposed the question put to me by a philosopher of the day, 'Why cannot you go your way, and let us go ours?' I answer, in the name of the Science of Religion, 'When Newton can dispense with metaphysics, then may you dispense with us.'"

19. Ibid., 46.

20. Ibid., 38.

fend it. Theology has some terms and methods of its own, but its fundamental tools are borrowed from philosophy.

The growth of religious fundamentalism and the collapse of religious education mean theology is more urgently needed in the universities—especially the Catholic ones—than ever before. This means students are uniquely dependent on theologians. Sadly, however, students are often not up to the hard thinking and arguing necessary to explain and support an idea like the Trinity or moral truth, or even the existence of God. Such topics are not just interesting theological tidbits. They are the hard reality of faith, the reason for believing at all. *Fides et ratio* teaches that a good theological grasp of them requires philosophical learning—and teaching them requires immense philosophical learning.

Consider a topic such as transubstantiation, or the Prologue to John's Gospel. No one could possibly understand the former without a good understanding of various views of substance and the arguments for and against them; and no one could explain the Prologue without some knowledge of the Greek and Hebrew philosophy of reason, concept, light, revelation, God. This is precisely what we should expect. If truth is a unity, as Newman claims, there is no truth "in religion" distinct from some truths "in fact" or "in philosophy." There is simply truth. The higher truths are rightly explained by theology, which is enabled to do what it does because of its basis in philosophical concepts and arguments.

As well as being essential to theological study, philosophy is an indispensable tool for communicating theology, for evangelization and catechesis. A faith based on how warm and comfortable you feel and how "affirmed" you are by your community is pleasant, but there is no guarantee that it is true. *Fides et ratio* makes clear that philosophy's central tasks are to justify our grasp of reality, of truth, and to make cogent suggestions as to life's true meaning. Being able to say something compelling on these topics—reality, truth, and life's meaning—is critical in winning young and old alike to the faith. A theology that incorporates philosophy's work in these areas will be faithful to the teaching of the Church and able to stand up to the most rigorous secular arguments and the ideologies of the age.

Many of the problems with university theology arise because the academic feels himself permitted or pressured to pursue intellectual fads and fashions. If he has little philosophical formation he will hold to the most comforting or popular theological position available and devise an appropriate "philosophy" of his own to support this. This is disastrous. The salvation of university theologians—and their students—depends upon their willingness to apply their critical skills to objective Church teachings and to think philosophically and not ideologically as they theologize. This deeply important piece of Catholic tradition, exemplified in Newman's own work on the relationship between faith and the university, is now confirmed in *Fides et ratio*.

Some, not least within the Church, have taken issue with *Fides et ratio* and its treatment of the relationship between theology and philosophy, and the implications this has for the university. Others, of course, unable to take issue with the intellectual giant that John Paul II was, simply ignore it. This is a pity, but no surprise. One of the silliest and thinnest claims advanced against John Paul II's wider reflections on faith and the university is that adoption of the approach he outlines would result in a suffocating conformity and close up the room for original and innovative work in all disciplines, and especially in theology. It could be said by uncharitable critics that the fruits of the last forty years of supposedly "original" and "innovative" work in Catholic theology have not been what was hoped for. But whatever of that, it is simply wrong to assume that faithfulness to the magisterium of the Church closes down debate and dialogue and makes new approaches impossible. Some of the most important theological and philosophical innovations over the last decades have come from the revived natural law tradition, led by first-rate minds such as John Finnis, Robert George, Mary Ann Glendon, and Germain Grisez, who are utterly faithful to the Church and who have made an enormous and original contribution to explaining and defending Christian claims to the wider world. The examples could be multiplied, but the point is clear enough: faithfulness is no obstacle to originality, although it may be for mediocrity.

Nor does faithfulness at the institutional level stifle a university's particular character and identity. Newman understood that every university, and every Catholic university, will be founded on "some particular form of the general idea that a university teaches universal knowledge. In this sense a university can never be 'uncommitted.'" The particular form this commitment takes will determine a university's particular identity.[21] There is an enormous range of piety, devotion, and spiritualities within the Catholic Church, and the "catholicity"—the universality—of orthodoxy also applies to Catholic universities. If one thing is clear from the developments within the Church over the last few decades, it is that fruitfulness belongs to orthodoxy. Just consider the New Lay Movements in the Church. There has been nothing remotely comparable on the liberal side of the arena. On the contrary, the groups and formations involved on that side of things all look very much the same, and very dated. Catholic universities should perhaps bear this lesson in mind. If they want to be different, if they want to do new things fruitfully, the precondition is to be faithful.

The famous speech Newman made in reply to receiving the *biglietto* informing him of his elevation to the College of Cardinals in 1878 set his own liberal Catholicism against a very different kind of religious liberalism, what he described in the *Apologia* as a "false liberty of thought."[22] His boast, as liberal cleric, was that "for thirty, forty, fifty years I have resisted to the best of my powers the spirit of liberalism in religion." As Father Ker remarks in his biography, "as the Cardinal-elect warmed to his theme, we hear very distinctly the voice of a younger Newman":

21. Ker, *John Henry Newman,* 389.
22. John Henry Newman, *Apologia Pro Vita Sua* (1865) (New York: Image Books, 1956), Part 4, 163.

Liberalism in religion is the doctrine that there is no positive truth in religion, but that one creed is as good as another, and this is the teaching which is gaining substance and force daily. It is inconsistent with any recognition of any religion as true. It teaches that all are to be tolerated, for all are matters of opinion. Revealed religion is not truth, but a sentiment or a taste; not an objective fact, not miraculous; and it is the right of each individual to make it say just what strikes his fancy.

There is much, Newman goes on, in the liberal approach to things "which is good and true: for example ... the precepts of justice, truthfulness, sobriety, self-command, benevolence, which ... are among its avowed principles, and the natural laws of society." But it is precisely because of the positive aspects of the liberal disposition that "there was never a device of the enemy, so cleverly framed, and with such promise of success."[23] In Catholic universities we need to recapture the liberal disposition and qualities that Newman extolled and personally exemplified, and to free ourselves from the straitjacket of ideological liberalism. On this basis, we might hope to see a new flowering of theology in the university.

23. Ker, *John Henry Newman*, 720–21.

10. HUMAN DIGNITY, HUMAN RIGHTS, AND MORAL RESPONSIBILITY

In his 1993 encyclical *Veritatis splendor* Pope John Paul II claimed that the Church was facing a genuine crisis that touched the very foundations of moral theology.[1] He explained that this crisis was no longer a matter of limited and occasional dissent but of an overall and systematic calling into question of traditional moral doctrine.[2]

It is a moot point whether the crisis has lessened or deepened in the years since *Veritatis splendor* was published, or indeed whether the situation remains basically as it was. Rome has spoken, but in the English-speaking world there is no evidence that the matter has been successfully concluded. I speak as an Australian bishop primarily about the situation in Australia. It remains for others to judge just how relevant my comments might be for the situation in the United States and other parts of the Catholic world.

After a few introductory words to set the scene I will focus on two topics central to human dignity and moral responsibility. One was treated extensively in *Veritatis splendor*—the role of conscience—and the second is the Christian understanding of human rights. I believe in both conscience and human rights, but I believe the doctrine of the primacy of conscience is incompatible not only

This chapter was originally an address to an International Symposium to mark the twenty-fifth anniversary of the pontificate of Pope John Paul II, St. Charles Borromeo Seminary Wynneward, Philadelphia, Pennsylvania, 4 October 2003, and was subsequently published in Kevin T. McMahon, S.T.D., ed., *Catholic Moral Teaching in the Pontificate of John Paul II* (Overbrook, PA: St. Charles Borremeo Seminary, The John Cardinal Krol Chair of Moral Theology, 2004).

1. John Paul II, Encyclical Letter *Veritatis splendor* (1993), §5.
2. Ibid., §4.

with the Christian concept of human rights, but with any concept of human rights.

THE PONTIFICATE OF JOHN PAUL II

Pope John Paul II was an historical anomaly. We risk categorizing his outstanding achievements as being normative for the papacy. This is particularly a danger for the generation of young Catholics who, until John Paul's death, knew no other pope. In fact no pope in history, even Pope John XXIII, has exercised such an influence in so many fields. This is partly a consequence of the mass media today, but more particularly it is a consequence of his unique contribution. *Veritatis splendor* was discussed everywhere throughout the Western world. The major papers in just about every Western capital city editorialized on this encyclical. John Paul's defense of human rights against communism and totalitarianism was pivotal. This is but one part of his extraordinary achievements. An important task for the future will be to assimilate his teachings and put them into practice.

This encyclical had been announced on the Feast of St. Alphonsus in 1987, but did not appear until after the publication of the *Catechism of the Catholic Church*. It was eagerly awaited by admirers of John Paul II and also by his opponents inside and outside the Catholic Church. The traditional loose alliance of dissidents were well organized with their allies in the secular media to orchestrate a chorus of dissent, as they had done so successfully in 1968 against Pope Paul VI's encyclical *Humanae vitae*.

However, the world had changed since 1968 in a number of significant ways. First of all the scope for dissent had enlarged immeasurably. In 1968 the arguments for individual judgment or private conscience were advanced on the topic of the new means of contraception, which it was alleged, with some justification, was disputed even within the Catholic tradition. Today what remains in dispute are the grounds for moral argumentation itself within the Catholic and indeed Christian tradition, and the controverted areas now include every area of sexual practice, and many issues that touch human life. Consequently there are also significant debates on marriage and family life. There has been no period in Church history where such a range of moral teachings has been rejected and the rejecters have continued to insist on remaining within the Church and aspiring to change Church teaching. Also there has probably been no period in Church history where so many have been able to do this without effective retribution. To my knowledge no bishop has taken up John Paul's recommendation in *Veritatis splendor* to take away the title *Catholic* from Catholic institutions that are deviating significantly from sound moral doctrine.[3]

In 1968 many in the Church were optimistic that the progressive reforms of the Second Vatican Council would soon bring wonderful fruits, and that dialogue with the world would be one of the means for this. *Humanae vitae* was a valuable corrective to this inflated optimism. The collapse of the Church, for example, in Holland and French-speaking Canada then lay in the future, as did the exodus of many priests and religious and the radical decline in vocations to the priesthood and religious life in many parts of the Church. Today we are much better aware of the consequences of the acid rain of modernity on Catholic communities, of our minority status as serious Christians everywhere in the English-speaking world, and of the damaging power of the neo-pagan world of communications. Probably too we are better aware of the fruits of internal dissent.

However, Pope John Paul II was an immensely more powerful influence than Pope Paul VI. Pope Paul was fated to lead the Church at an intensely difficult time, but he will not rank with Leo the Great or Gregory the Great. John Paul II will, and one major reason for this will be his moral teaching, especially as outlined in *Veritatis splendor* and *Evangelium vitae* (1995).

3. Ibid., §116.

NO PRIMACY OF CONSCIENCE

Sections 54 to 64 of *Veritatis splendor* are the best short piece written on conscience since Cardinal Newman's *Letter to the Duke of Norfolk* in 1875. It is a sophisticated and accessible piece of work, quoting section 16 of the Second Vatican Council's Constitution on the Church in the Modern World, *Gaudium et spes* (1965), about the voice of conscience always summoning us to love good and avoid evil: "For man has in his heart a law written by God. To obey it is the very dignity of man; according to it he will be judged (cf. Rom 2:14–16)." There is an explicit reference to the development in the Church's moral doctrine similar to the development in the doctrines of faith, provided the original meaning is preserved intact.[4] The encyclical is not fundamentalist.

Naturally I accept the teaching of the Second Vatican Council and *Veritatis splendor* on the crucial role of conscience for us all. However, for some years I have spoken and written against the so-called doctrine of the primacy of conscience, arguing that this is incompatible with traditional Catholic teaching. Not surprisingly, this has in turn provoked a number of hostile public refutations and quite a number of letters from friends and acquaintances attempting to persuade me of the error of my ways.

My basic object is twofold: (1) to explain that increasingly, even in Catholic circles, the appeal to the primacy of conscience is being used to justify what we would like to do rather than to discover what God wants us to do; and (2) to claim that conscience does not have primacy. One should say that the word of God has primacy or that truth has primacy, and that a person uses his conscience to discern the truth in particular cases. Individual conscience cannot confer the right to reject or distort New Testament morality as affirmed or developed by the Church. To use the language of *Veritatis splendor*, conscience is "the proximate norm of personal morality," whose authority in its voice and judgment "derives from the truth about moral good and evil."[5]

4. Ibid., §54 and n100.   5. Ibid., §60.

Whatever the pressures for conformity produced by public opinion and the mass media today, there is a healthy rhetoric about respect for the rights of the individual, including the right to private judgment, in the English-speaking democracies. Today we value freedom of speech, however much it might have been constrained in the distant past. We take it for granted that all citizens have a freedom to choose their career and their home, and all adults presume unreflectingly the right to choose a spouse—or now, increasingly in Australia, a temporary partner. Just as people have the right in a democracy to choose their religion, so too some Catholics feel they should be able to choose the type of morality they follow and remain "good" Catholics.

Unless all kinds of implicit Christian assumptions are made explicit, the claim to the primacy of individual conscience easily becomes in our cultural context the same as a claim to personal moral autonomy. Indeed most Western moral philosophers since the eighteenth century, with the exceptions of the Marxists and the Christians, have followed Kant in advocating some form of moral self-legislation and government (autonomy), as distinct from heteronomy or rule by others. Even Kant would be appalled by contemporary autonomy liberalism. He believed in objective morality ("practical reason"), which autonomy gives us the means and opportunity to follow, never a self-made morality of private preference.[6]

When a person is autonomous, or independent, or at liberty to follow his will in moral matters, this implies that other persons have some kind of obligation to respect this person's freedom of judgment and action. What is the nature of the obligation of other people toward the agent? We might look at this from another perspective and ask: what is the extent of the agent's freedom to follow his own will? In response one can usefully give two versions of moral autonomy. The first emphasizes the person's right to choose in the areas of life generally open to moral evaluation, leaving the limits outside which the agent might curtail his right generally unspecified.

6. Immanuel Kant, *The Metaphysics of Morals* (1797), trans. Mary Gregor (Cambridge: Cambridge University Press, 1991), 40–53.

John Rawls has defined the extreme of this version of autonomy with characteristic lucidity. It is "the complete freedom to
form our moral opinions so that the conscientious judgment of
every moral agent ought absolutely to be respected."[7] The realities of social life and public order constrain us into recognizing
the impracticalities of such a principle as a basis for our personal conduct. In any society the only two alternatives are unanimity or the exercise of authority. The second version of autonomy, the more practical version, always spells out in some way the
constraints necessary for social life. The principle of autonomy
that informs Rawls's own work, his alternative and more practical
meaning, defines acting autonomously as "acting from principles
that we would consent to as free and equal rational beings."[8] I am
not arguing this account is adequate, merely that it is one example
of the limitations and precisions required.

Those Catholics who appeal to the primacy of conscience cite
a number of classical references. The first comes from the Second
Vatican Council's Declaration on Religious Freedom, *Dignitatis humanae* (1965), which states that religious freedom "has to do with
immunity from coercion in civil society"; "The truth cannot impose itself except by virtue of its own truth." However, these advocates often leave unsaid the conciliar teaching from the same
paragraph that religious freedom "leaves untouched traditional
Catholic doctrine on the moral duty of men in society towards
the true religion and towards the one Church of Christ."[9] So while
the Declaration explains that in matters religious "no man is to be
forced to act in a manner contrary to his own beliefs . . . within due
limits," it also goes on to say that all men are "bound by a moral
obligation to seek the truth, especially religious truth."[10]

Father John Courtney Murray, S.J., who had such a profound

7. Rawls, *A Theory of Justice*, 518.
8. Ibid., 516.
9. Second Vatican Council, Declaration on Religious Freedom, *Dignitatis
humanae* (1965), §1.
10. Ibid., §2.

influence in the production of *Dignitatis humanae*, wrote in his introduction to the English translation: "The conciliar affirmation of the principle of freedom was narrowly limited—in the text. But the text itself was flung into a pool whose shores are wide as the Universal Church. The ripples will run far. Inevitably, a great second argument will be set afoot—now on the theological meaning of Christian freedom."[11] In other words *Dignitatis humanae* speaks of relationships between state and Church, and between the state and individual. It does not deal with the relationship between the magisterium and the baptized.

A second reference frequently quoted, and indeed cited by John Paul II himself in *Crossing the Threshold of Hope*, comes from St. Thomas Aquinas, who explains that if a man is admonished by his conscience, even when it is erroneous he must always listen to it and follow it.[12] The supporters of primacy of conscience do not go on to explain, as Aquinas does and John Paul II did over a lifetime of writing, that the binding force of conscience, even mistaken conscience, comes from the person's belief that the conscientious decision is in accord with the law of God.[13] I also believe that a person following Aquinas's advice not only might err in an objective sense, but could be guilty for his mistaken views. But more on this later.

A final passage, also frequently cited, is Cardinal Newman's famous declaration at the end of his *Letter to the Duke of Norfolk:* "Certainly, if I am obliged to bring religion into after-dinner toasts (which indeed does not seem quite the thing) I shall drink—to the Pope, if you please—still, to Conscience first, and to the Pope afterwards."[14] Newman was concerned about the ultramontane

11. John Courtney Murray, S.J., ed., *The Documents of Vatican II*, gen. ed. William M. Abbot, S.J. (London and Dublin: Chapman, 1966), 674.

12. John Paul II, *Crossing the Threshold of Hope* (London: Jonathan Cape, 1994), 191.

13. St. Thomas Aquinas, *Summa theologiae* (1–2, 19, 5). See also the Commentary in *Epistolam ad Romanos* (14, 2, ad 5).

14. John Henry Newman, *Letter to the Duke of Norfolk* (1875), in *The Genius of John Henry Newman: Selections from His Writings*, ed. Ian Ker (Oxford: Clarendon Press, 1989), 267.

claims of extreme infallibilists, facetiously explaining that if the pope told the English bishops to order their priests to work for teetotalism or to hold a lottery in each mission, they would not be obliged to do so. But there is no doubt also that his understanding of conscience is very specifically Christocentric and God-centered, within the Catholic tradition.

Conscience is not a long-sighted selfishness, nor a desire to be consistent with oneself; but it is a messenger from Him, who, both in nature and in grace, speaks to us behind a veil, and teaches and rules us by His representatives. Conscience is the aboriginal Vicar of Christ, a prophet in its informations, a monarch in its peremptoriness, a priest in its blessings and anathemas, and even though the eternal priesthood throughout the Church should cease to be, in it the sacerdotal principle would remain and would have a sway.[15]

In all Newman's examples, conscience is not left as an unfenced equivalent of secular autonomy but is closely defined and linked with a proper understanding of Christian, and indeed Catholic, teaching.

In strictly theological language the claim to primacy of conscience is a cliché, which requires only preliminary examination for us to conclude that it needs to be refined and developed to have any plausible meaning at all. I do not even favor the substitution of the primacy of *informed* conscience, because it is also possible that with good will and conscientious study a devout Catholic could fail to recognize some moral truth and act upon this failure. It is truth, or the word of God, that has primacy, and we have to use our personal capacity to reason practically, that is, exercise our conscience, to try to recognize these particular truths.

While occasionally at the theological level I feel that all I am doing is forcing my way through an open door, it is at the pastoral level that this espousal of the primacy of conscience has disastrous effect. Let me give you a crass but actual example, recounted to me by a friend who witnessed this encounter. A man asked a

15. Ibid., 263–64. Cf. *Catechism of the Catholic Church* (1994), §1778.

question: "Suppose I have been regularly sleeping with my girl-friend. Would it be wrong for me to be receiving Holy Communion?" Without hesitation the theologian replied, "Vatican II has taught that in answering any moral question, you must obey your conscience. Just do that." Such a teaching is insufficient and misleading. Does it mean there are no moral absolutes or authorities? Is it sufficient to follow one's feelings? Or was Charlie Brown correct forty years ago to claim that "it doesn't matter what you believe as long as you're sincere"?

In many places, even in the Catholic world, the category of mortal, or death-bearing, sin is now an endangered species, because the unthinking presumption is that everyone is honestly doing his or her "own thing." Obviously public opinion places limits to this world of easy options, often coterminous with the limits of political correctness, but many areas of sexual conduct and activities such as contraception, abortion, euthanasia, and the number of children are "free go" areas, where one opinion is held to be as good as another.

This reflects the fact that there has been a dramatic shift in the tectonic plates of public moral discourse within the Catholic Church, and certainly within the ranks of the other Christian churches. The public disarray in the Anglican churches on the suitability of ordaining active homosexual men and women to the Anglican ministry is one spectacular example of this.

Once upon a time it was pastorally useful, sometimes necessary, to explain the possibility of invincible ignorance among those who differed from us, because of the temptation to presume bad faith in opponents. Now for many tolerance is the first and most important commandment. Now it is necessary and important for us to argue for the possibility of culpable ignorance, indeed the possibility of culpable ignorance that usually has been built up through years of sin and is psychologically invincible, short of a miracle. The idea of culpable moral blindness is discussed as infrequently as the pains of hell.

Jesus knew human nature very well, and *Veritatis splendor* quotes that marvelous saying of Our Lord from St. Matthew's Gospel: "The eye is the lamp of the body. So if your eye is sound, your whole body will be full of light; but if your eye is not sound, your whole body will be full of darkness. If then the light in you is darkness, how great is the darkness!"[16]

Christian writers at different times have expounded wonderfully on the concept of culpable moral blindness. St. Thomas More wrote his *Dialogue of Comfort against Tribulation* in the final year of his imprisonment in the Tower of London, speaking there of conscience's susceptibility to corruption whether by the cynicism and self-love of Father Renard (Father Fox) and Master Wolf or by conscientious blindness through the stupidity of poor scrupulous Master Ass.[17]

Even earlier, in 1377–78, St. Catherine of Sienna in her *Dialogue* spoke of the consequences of pride, sensuality, and impatience and the consequent lack of discernment. These four chief vices constitute a tree of death. "Within these trees a worm of conscience nibbles. But as long as a person lives in deadly sin the worm is blinded and is so little felt."[18]

CHRISTIANITY AND HUMAN RIGHTS

The great saints and doctors of the Church I have quoted to demonstrate that conscience lives under the truth and has to take its bearings from it were not afraid of using godly language to make this clear. This was also true of Pope John Paul II. There has been a tendency, at least in Australia, and not just among Catholic intellectuals but also among bishops and priests, to make the public argument for Catholic moral claims and social teaching on the basis of

16. Mt 6:22–23.

17. St. Thomas More, *Dialogue of Comfort against Tribulation* (1535) (London: Sheed and Ward, 1951), 93–98. Quoted in John Finnis, "Address to the Thomas More Society," Melbourne, 23 August 1999.

18. St. Catherine of Siena, *The Dialogue* (1337–38), (New York: Paulist Press, 1980), §31.

secular reason, without too much reference to God. Relying on this approach too much can be a mistake. I think we should follow the example of St. Thomas More and St. Catherine of Siena and make God a central part of the case we make to the world.

As someone who believes, even apart from revelation, that it is more reasonable to be a theist than an atheist or agnostic, and in societies where 80 or 90 percent of the population believes in God, we should not concede that secularism is the only basis for public discourse, and we should never accept that Catholic discourse be described as "sectarian" or "partisan."

Not surprisingly, the moral muddle that people find themselves in at the personal level on questions of conscience and autonomy has important consequences at the public level. The Australian moral theologian Tracey Rowland has argued strongly that the reluctance to use godly language and the explicit language of the Catholic tradition when addressing the common good has not helped this confusion, and may very well have made it worse. Rowland argues that using secular language to set out Catholic claims does not persuade secularists and only serves to mislead the faithful by suggesting an agreement in substance that does not exist and that makes it easier for Catholics to accept a secular understanding of autonomy and freedom, especially when it comes to the hard teachings of the Gospel.[19] Clearly, a greater use of godly language in making the Catholic case to the world would be significant step toward rectifying this situation.

There are some in the Church (and Rowland, following Alasdair MacIntyre and David Schindler, is among them) who argue that Catholics should not use (what MacIntyre calls) the "dubious idiom and rhetoric of rights" regnant in Western democracy, either as a basis for dialogue with secularists or as a vehicle for advancing the Catholic understanding of justice, morality, and the common good.[20] Attempting to do this fails to take account of the way

19. Rowland, *Culture and the Thomist Tradition after Vatican II*, 156.
20. Ibid., 148.

the secular liberal tradition developed in opposition to the classical Christian synthesis and the anthropological assumptions that sustain it.[21] The danger in pursuing this course, so it is argued, is that we will gain nothing (because secular liberals will not abandon their secularism simply because we appeal to their liberalism) and lose everything (by inadvertently encouraging recourse to secular understandings of the person, freedom, and autonomy among the faithful). But while these critics' identification of this danger is not entirely misplaced, it is exaggerated. We need to keep a sense of perspective and to remember that while ideas certainly have consequences, the logic they follow in working themselves out rarely proceeds in academic purity.

We are all aware of the enormous secular pressure on the Church to mind its own spiritual and religious business, and to leave the question of which values the community should adopt to those who can consider it in an "unbiased" (that is, *secular*) fashion. This is not a position that the Church can ever accept. In *Veritatis splendor* John Paul II cited the Code of Canon Law to make this abundantly clear, declaring that "the Church has the right always and everywhere to proclaim moral principles, even in respect of the social order, and to make judgments about any human matter in so far as this is required by fundamental human rights or the salvation of souls."[22] Note the grounds on which the Church bases its interventions in the public domain: the salvation of souls and the defense of fundamental human rights. While language such as "the salvation of souls" is not much in vogue in Australia (something we should rectify), one of the many ways in which the Church serves this good today is precisely through the defense of fundamental human rights. For John Paul II, abandoning the idea of human rights is not an option.

A dramatic example of this was provided in *Evangelium vitae* when John Paul II referred to indications suggesting "an objective

21. Ibid., 157.
22. *Veritatis splendor*, §29, citing Canon 747, 2.

conspiracy against life"[23] and against the most fundamental right of all: the right to life. On the one hand, John Paul observed, we have "the various declarations of human rights ... [and] a growing moral sensitivity, more alert to acknowledging the value and dignity of every human being, without any distinction." But on the other hand, "these noble proclamations" and sentiments are "contradicted by a tragic repudiation of them in practice." This poses *"a direct threat to the entire culture of human rights."*[24] When we consider that "many countries, perhaps even departing from basic principles of their Constitutions," have determined not to punish destructive practices against life "and even to make them legal,"[25] the threat posed to the entire culture of human rights cannot be mistaken for some sort of intellectual abstraction.

The analogue to the primacy of conscience in the private domain is found in what might be called "the primacy of rights" in the public domain. Just as conscience is claimed to have primacy over truth, rights are claimed to have primacy over *justice,* in the full sense of that word as it understood in the Catholic tradition. In both cases there is an assertion of the self against truth and against other people, to the detriment of both conscience and rights. In *Evangelium vitae* John Paul II warned that the threat posed by human rights turning against themselves in this way particularly endangers the rights of the weakest, and is capable "in the end, of jeopardizing the very meaning of democratic coexistence."[26] This concern is foreshadowed in *Veritatis splendor* when we are reminded that "only a morality which acknowledges certain norms as valid always and for everyone, with no exception, can guarantee the ethical foundation of social coexistence," nationally and internationally.[27] A culture of rights needs to be soundly based on justice. It is doubtful that the relativist and positivist concepts of justice that predominate today can provide this.

23. *Evangelium vitae,* §17.
24. Ibid., §18.
25. Ibid., §4.
26. Ibid., §18.
27. *Veritatis splendor,* §97.

Veritatis splendor emphasizes *"the risk of an alliance between democracy and ethical relativism,* which would remove any sure moral reference point from political and social life, and on a deeper level, make the acknowledgement of truth impossible." It repeats the words of *Centesimus annus* (1991) tracing the violation of human rights to "the denial of the transcendent dignity of the human person" and warning against "a democracy without values," which easily becomes "open or thinly disguised totalitarianism."[28] John Paul observes that in the face of "fundamental human rights [being] trampled upon and held in contempt" there is a "widespread and acute sense of *the need for a radical* personal and social *renewal* capable of ensuring justice, solidarity, honesty and openness."[29] The basis for this renewal, and "the unshakeable foundation and essential condition of morality," human rights, justice, and "the personal dignity of man" can be found only in the truth: "the truth of God, the Creator and Redeemer, and the truth of man, created and redeemed by him."[30]

"What is truth?"[31] Pilate's derisive question to Our Lord was regarded by Nietzsche as the only insight of any value in the whole New Testament.[32] In the postmodern world of the West that Nietzsche did so much to bring about, Pilate's question is increasingly thrown in the face of the Church as well, sometimes searchingly but more often than not with cynicism and condescension. This incident in the Passion reflects our own situation too, where power sits in judgment on truth and finds it worthy only of condemnation. The arguments against truth take the form of a cas-

---

28. Ibid., §§99 and 101. Cf. John Paul II, Encyclical Letter *Centesimus annus* (1991), §§44 and 46.

29. *Veritatis splendor,* §98.   30. Ibid., §99.

31. Jn 18:38.

32. Friedrich Nietzsche, *The Anti-Christ* (1889), in *The Anti-Christ, Ecce Homo, Twilight of the Idols and Other Writings,* ed. Aaron Ridley and Judith Norman, trans. Judith Norman (Cambridge: Cambridge University Press, 2005), 45: "The noble scorn of a Roman when faced with an unashamed mangling of the word 'truth' gave the New Testament its only statement *of any value,*—its critique, even its *annihilation:* 'What is truth!'"

cade designed to ensure that it is ruled out of consideration one
way or another: there is no such thing as truth; or if there is, we
cannot know it with certainty; or if we can, we cannot agree about
it. Best then to forget about this problem. Our purported inabil-
ity to know and live the truth places only one demand before us,
that we be tolerant of the views of others. But in the absence of
any genuine knowledge about what is intrinsically good or right,
tolerance becomes merely one value among many, of equal dignity
in fact with intolerance. This helps to explain why what is sometimes described as liberal tolerance so often serves as "a seminary
of intolerance" (in Leo Strauss's apt phrase), especially when it is
confronted by values or claims that might impede "the uninhibited
cultivation of individuality."[33]

In the absence of truth, on what basis do we give preference
to upholding human rights over trampling them underfoot? There
is no basis, of course. We simply have to make a decision one way
or the other. For some theorists this is sufficient. At one extreme
there is the German legal theorist Carl Schmitt, who argued that
the essential thing is the decision: it does not matter what you decide for, as long as a decision is made and adhered to resolutely
until the end.[34] At the other extreme there is the American philosopher Richard Rorty, who argues that not only is there no truth
to guide us in the consideration of equally valid choices, but that
the "truth" of a choice adds nothing to it. Truth is not needed, for
once a decision has been made, we live it out in any case "as if" it
were true. It is decision, not truth, that animates action, and while
Rorty would prefer that we make our decision in favor of his own
secular liberal values, this applies irrespective of whether we decide
to respect or violate human rights.[35]

This idea of "decisionism" (as others have called it) is drawn

33. Leo Strauss, *Natural Right and History* (1950) (Chicago: University of Chicago Press, 1965), 5–6.

34. Carl Schmitt, *The Concept of the Political* (1932), trans. George Schwab (1975) (Chicago: University of Chicago Press, 1996).

35. Rorty, *Contingency, Irony, and Solidarity*.

upon in different guises as a way of showing how political and social action might be sustained in a situation of radical ethical relativism. In a democracy Rorty is likely to have greater appeal on
this score than Schmitt with his particular historical associations,
but Schmitt is perhaps the more instructive case for understanding where this approach can lead. The crucial question is whether
a mere decision, even a deadly serious decision, in favor of human
rights is sufficient to sustain the commitment and action necessary to ensure that rights are consistently respected. Leo Strauss,
for one, suggests that a decision is not enough: "Once we realize that the principles of our actions have no other support than
blind choice, we really do not believe in them any more. We cannot
wholeheartedly act upon them any more. We cannot live any more
as responsible beings. In order to live, we have to silence the easily
silenced voice of reason, which tells us that our principles are in
themselves as good or bad as any other principles." If we are unable to find a foundation for the defense of conscience and human
rights in reason and truth, our commitment to both can be based
only on "fanatical obscurantism,"[36] although obviously we are unlikely to call it by this name.

The denial of truth makes impossible an enduring concept
of justice that genuinely serves human life and love. It makes, in
short, for nihilism. The practical meaning of this can be seen in
the contradiction John Paul II identifies between a growing aware-
ness of human rights and a repudiation of the fundamental rights
of some of the most vulnerable members of the human family.
We are so familiar with talk of the "right" to an abortion that it
can be difficult for us to recall what a shocking and absurd debase-
ment of the language of rights this is. And now, as medical science
continually pushes back the age at which premature babies can be
saved, including babies who have survived abortion, abortion activists are beginning to insist that abortion is not just the "right"
to terminate a pregnancy, but the "right" to "the extinction of the

36. Strauss, *Natural Right and History*, 6.

fetus."[37] When upholding human rights entails the assertion of the self against others, the entire culture of rights central to democracy is, as John Paul says, directly threatened. This strongly suggests that without a firm foundation in the transcendent dignity of the human person and the existence of moral absolutes that place limits on the human will, it becomes harder and harder for people to believe in, and maintain a wholehearted commitment to, human rights in all their fullness.

To refuse to use the language of rights and conscience in a situation where the secular understanding of rights is beginning to collapse under the weight of its own contradictions would only deny the Church an opportunity to reclaim some ground for an authentic understanding of the person, human freedom, and the common good. It is not too far-fetched to suggest that the collapse of the secular understanding of human rights raises the prospect of the whole idea of rights disappearing, especially as ideas that are more and more frankly Nietzschean push liberal presuppositions aside.[38] For the Church to do nothing to salvage and redeem the language of rights, precisely when the assertion of the self against others is becoming more brutal and the confrontation between power and truth is becoming more clear, would not only be counterproductive. It would also be a betrayal of the transcendent dignity and destiny of the person that John Paul II so powerfully recommitted the Church to defend.

CONCLUSION

John Paul II was right when, in his Angelus address of 17 August 2003, he claimed that "the Christian faith gave form [to Europe], and some of its fundamental values in turn inspired the democratic ideal and human rights of European modernity."

Human rights discourse properly understood can be used by

---

37. Sacha Zimmerman, "Fetal Position," *New Republic*, 18 and 25 August 2003.
38. Cf. Rowland, *Culture and the Thomist Tradition*, 155 and 158.

Catholics as a grammar for expressing, rather than diluting, our understanding of duties, especially those owed to the weak. But just as the *scientia* in conscience, knowing objective truth, has been replaced by preferences, feelings, and the invention and construction of moral obligations or options, so too human rights divorced from a proper understanding of the dignity of all persons can be used to further the culture of death and damage the civilization of life and love.

Pope John Paul II, especially in *Veritatis splendor* and *Evangelium vitae*, has made an invaluable contribution to this long struggle in which we are privileged to participate, not least by reminding us and underscoring the unbreakable linkage between God, truth, and freedom.

BIBLIOGRAPHY

Appleyard, Bryan. *Understanding the Present.* London: Picador, 1993.

Aquinas, Thomas. *Commentary on Aristotle's Nicomachean Ethics.* Trans. C. I. Litzinger. Notre Dame, IN: Dumb Ox Books, 1993.

Australian Bureau of Statistics. Canberra. *Australian Demographic Statistics,* December 2005.

————. *Australian Social Trends 2002.*

————. *Births, Australia 2000.*

————. *Census, Australia 2001.*

————. *Divorces, Australia 2003.*

————. *Marriages and Divorces, Australia 1999.*

————. *Suicides, Australia 1921–1998.*

————. *Suicides, Australia 1994–2004.*

Australian Catholic Bishops Conference, Pastoral Projects Office. National Attendance Count 2001. 2002.

Australian Community Survey. Sydney: NCLS Research, 1998.

Australian Social Monitor 3:1 (July 2000).

Australian Wellbeing and Security Survey. Sydney: Anglicare, 2002.

Baylor Religion Survey. Waco, TX: Baylor University, 2006.

Beer, Gavin de, ed. *Charles Darwin and Thomas Huxley: Autobiographies.* New York: Oxford University Press, 1974.

Behe, Michael J. *Darwin's Black Box: The Biochemical Challenge to Evolution.* New York: Free Press, 1996.

Bendix, Reinhard. *Max Weber: An Intellectual Portrait.* London: Methuen, 1966.

Berlin, Isaiah. *The Proper Study of Mankind.* Ed. Henry Hardy. New York: Farrar, Straus and Giroux, 1998.

Berman, Harold J. *Law and Revolution: The Formation of the Western Legal Tradition.* Cambridge MA: Harvard University Press, 1983.

Brunton, Ron. *The End of the Overpopulation Crisis?* Melbourne: Institute of Public Affairs, 1998.

Carlson, Allan C. "Sweden and the Failure of European Family Policy." *Society* 42:6 (September–October 2005): 41–46.

Casey, M. A. "Authority, Crisis, and the Individual." *Society* 39:2 (January–February 2002): 78–82.

————. *Meaninglessness: The Solutions of Nietzsche, Freud and Rorty.* Lanham, MD: Lexington, 2001.

————. "The Politics of Meaninglessness." *Sydney Papers* 15:3–4 (Winter–Spring 2003): 136–43.

Catechism of the Catholic Church. 1994.

Catherine of Siena. *The Dialogue* (1337–38). New York: Paulist Press, 1980.

Center for the Study of Global Christianity. *World Christian Database.* www.world
christiandatabase.org.

Chadwick, Owen. *The Secularization of the European Mind in the Nineteenth Century.*
Cambridge: Cambridge University Press, 1975.

Christian Research Association. *Australia's Religious Communities.* 2nd ed.
Melbourne: Christian Research Association, 2004.

Clark, Randall Baldwin. "Platonic Love in a Colorado Court Room: Martha
Nussbaum, John Finnis, and Plato's *Laws* in *Evans v. Romer.*" *Yale Journal of
Law and Humanities* 12 (2000): 1–38.

Congregation for the Doctrine of the Faith. "Letter to the Bishops of the
Catholic Church on the Pastoral Care of Homosexual Persons." 1986.

————. *Libertatis conscientia,* Instruction On Christian Freedom and Liberation.
1986.

————. *Libertatis nuntius,* Instruction On Certain Aspects of the "Theology of
Liberation." 1984.

Conquest, Robert. *Harvest of Sorrow: Soviet Collectivization and the Terror-Famine.* New
York: Oxford University Press, 1986.

Corwin E. S. *Corwin on the Constitution.* Ed. Richard Loss. Cornell University
Press: London, 1981.

Cotton, Catherine, and David Cotton, eds. *Abortion in Australia into the Twenty-
First Century: Facts, Current Trends, and a Way Ahead.* Sydney: New South Wales
Right to Life, 2006.

Courtois, Stéphane, et al., eds. *The Black Book of Communism* (1997). Ed. Mark
Kramer. Trans. Jonathan Murphy. Cambridge, MA: Harvard University
Press, 1999.

Culliford, Larry. "Spirituality and Clinical Care." *British Journal of Medicine* 325
(21–28 December 2002): 1434–35.

Dalberg-Acton, John Emerich Edward. "Inaugural Lecture on the Study of
History" (1885). In *Selected Writings of Lord Acton.* Vol. 2: *Essays in the Study and
Writing of History.* Ed. J. Rufus Fears. Indianapolis IN: Liberty Classics,
1987.

"Darwin Wins." *Time,* 18 January 1982.

Davies, Paul. *The Mind of God: The Scientific Basis for a Rational World.* New York:
Simon and Schuster, 1992.

Dulles, Avery, S.J. *The Reshaping of Catholicism.* San Francisco: Harper and Row,
1988.

Duncan, David Ewing. *The Calendar.* London: Fourth Estate, 1998.

Eastland, Larry L. "The Empty Cradle Will Rock." *Wall Street Journal,* 28 June
2004.

Eberstadt, Nicholas. "Too Few People?" *Prospect* 25 (December 1997): 50–55.

Elshtain, Jean Bethke. "Democratic Authority at Century's End." *Hedgehog Review* 2:1 (Spring 2000): 24–39.

————. "The Bright Line: Liberalism and Religion." *New Criterion* 17:7 (March 1999): 4–13.

Fernández-Armesto, Felipe. "America Can Still Save the World." *Spectator,* 8 January 2000.

Finnis, John. "Address to the Thomas More Society." Melbourne, 23 August 1999.

————. "Law, Morality, and 'Sexual Orientation.'" *Notre Dame Law Review* 69 (1994): 1049–76

————. *Natural Law and Natural Rights.* Oxford: Clarendon Press, 1980.

Fisher, Anthony, O.P., and Hayden Ramsay, eds. *Faith and Reason: Friends or Foes in the New Millennium?* Adelaide: ATF Press, 2004.

Franklin, Roger. "The Spirit of Woodstock on the Eve of Destruction." *Sunday Age,* 1 August 1999.

"Freedom of Belief." Editorial. *Sydney Morning Herald,* 21 August 2001.

Gartenstein-Ross, Daveed. "Legislating Religious Correctness." *Weekly Standard,* 27 October 2005.

George, Robert P. *Making Men Moral: Civil Liberties and Public Morality.* Oxford: Clarendon Press, 1993.

Glendon, Mary Ann. *A World Made New: Eleanor Roosevelt and the Universal Declaration of Human Rights.* New York: Random House, 2001.

Gray, John. "Two Liberalisms of Fear." *Hedgehog Review* 2:1 (Spring 2000): 9–23.

Haldane, John. "The Diversity of Philosophy and the Unity of its Vocation." In *Faith and Reason: Friends or Foes in the New Millennium,* ed. Anthony Fisher, O.P., and Hayden Ramsay. Adelaide: ATF Press, 2004.

————. "A Return to Form in Philosophy." In *Form and Matter: Themes in Contemporary Metaphysics,* ed. David Oderberg. Malden, MA: Blackwells, 1999.

Hall, Daniel E. "Religious Attendance: More Cost-Effective than Lipitor?" *Journal of the American Board of Family Medicine* 19:2 (March 2006): 103–9.

Harris, William S., and Manohar Gowda. "A Randomized, Controlled Trial of the Effects of Remote Intercessory Prayer on Outcomes in Patients Admitted to the Coronary Care Unit." *Archives of Internal Medicine* 159:19 (25 October 1999): 2273–78.

Hewitt, Belinda, Janeen Baxter, and Mark Western. "Marriage Breakdown in Australia: The Social Correlates of Separation and Divorce." *Journal of Sociology* 41 (June 2005): 163–83.

Himmelfarb, Gertrude. "Democratic Remedies for Democratic Disorders." *Public Interest* 131 (Spring 1998): 3–24.

————. "The Ghost of Parson Malthus." *Times Literary Supplement,* 23 January 1999.

Hittinger, Russell. "Abortion before Roe." *First Things* 46 (October 1994): 14–16.

————. "What Is Man?" *First Things* 88 (December 1998): 42–44.

Hughes, Philip. "Trends in Religious Identification: Details from the 2001 Census." *Pointers: Bulletin of the Christian Research Association* 12:3 (September 2002): 1–4.

Hume, David. *An Enquiry Concerning Human Understanding* (1748). In L. A. Selby-Bigge, ed., *Enquiries Concerning Human Understanding and Concerning the Principles of Morals* (1902). 3rd ed. rev. P. H. Nidditch. Oxford: Oxford University Press, 1975.

————. *Dialogues Concerning Natural Religion* (1779). Ed. J. C. A. Gaskin. Oxford: Oxford University Press, 1993.

————. *Four Dissertations* (1757). Bristol: Thoemmes Press, 1997.

Hummer, Robert A., et al. "Religious Involvement and US Adult Mortality." *Demography* 36:2 (May 1999): 273–85.

John Paul II. "Address to the 50th General Assembly of the United Nations." New York, 5 October 1995.

————. *Crossing the Threshold of Hope.* London: Jonathan Cape, 1994.

————. Encyclical Letter *Centesimus annus.* 1991.

————. Encyclical Letter *Evangelium vitae.* 1995.

————. Encyclical Letter *Fides et ratio.* 1998.

————. Encyclical Letter *Veritatis splendor.* 1993.

————. *The Theology of the Body.* Boston: Pauline Books, 1997.

Johnson, Paul. *The Quest for God.* London: Harper Collins, 1996.

Kamenka, Eugene. *The Philosophy of Ludwig Feuerbach.* London: Routledge and Kegan Paul, 1970.

Kant, Immanuel. *The Metaphysics of Morals* (1797). Trans. Mary Gregor. Cambridge: Cambridge University Press, 1991.

Ker, Ian. *John Henry Newman: A Biography.* Oxford: Clarendon Press, 1988.

Klusendorf, Scott. "The Vanishing Pro-Life Activist." *Christian Research Journal* 22:1 (Fall 1999): 23–25 and 42–45.

Koenig, Harold G. "Religion, Spirituality and Health: An American Physician's Response." *Medical Journal of Australia* 178:2 (20 January 2003): 51–52.

Koenig, Harold G., et al. "Does Religious Attendance Prolong Survival?" *Journals of Gerontology. Series A, Biological Sciences and Medical Sciences* 54:7 (July 1999): M370–M376.

Koenig, Harold G., Michael E. McCullough, and David B. Larson. *Handbook of Religion and Health.* Oxford: Oxford University Press: 2001.

Lawler, Peter Augustine. "Communism Today." *Society* 41:4 (May–June 2004): 24–30.

Locke, John. *An Essay Concerning Human Understanding* (1690). Ed. Peter H. Nidditch. Oxford: Clarendon Press, 1975.

Longman, Phillip. *The Empty Cradle.* New York: Perseus Books, 2004.

MacIntyre, Alasdair. "Community, Law, and the Idiom and Rhetoric of Rights." *Listening* 24:2 (1991): 96–110.

Maley, Barry. *Family and Marriage in Australia*. St. Leonards: Centre for Independent Studies, 2001.

Manent, Pierre. *The City of Man* (1994). Trans. Marc A. LePain. Princeton, NJ: Princeton University Press, 1998.

Maritain, Jacques. *Christianity and Democracy* (1943). In *Christian Democracy and The Rights of Man and Natural Law*. Trans. Doris C. Anson. San Francisco: Ignatius Press, 1986.

Mason, Michael, et al. "The Spirit of Generation Y: The Final Report of a Three Year Study." Unpublished report to project sponsors, 2006.

McCullough, Michael E., et al. "Religious Involvement and Mortality: A Meta-Analytic Review." *Health Psychology* 19:3 (May 2000): 211–22.

McGrath, Alister. *Dawkins' God: Genes, Memes and the Meaning of Life*. Oxford: Blackwells, 2005.

Midgley, E. B. F. *The Ideology of Max Weber: A Thomist Critique*. Lanham, MD: Rowman and Littlefield, 1983.

Millbank, John. "The Gift of Ruling: Secularization and Political Authority." *New Blackfriars* 996 (March 2004): 212–38.

Mol, Hans. *Religion in Australia*. Melbourne: Nelson, 1971.

More, Thomas. *Dialogue of Comfort against Tribulation* (1535). London: Sheed and Ward, 1951.

Morgan, Patricia. *Marriage Lite*. London: Institute for the Study of Civil Society, 2000.

Morson, Gary Saul. "How Did Dostoyevsky Know?" *New Criterion* 17:9 (May 1999): 21–30.

Murray, John Courtney, S.J., ed. *The Documents of Vatican II*. Gen. ed. William M. Abbot, S.J. London and Dublin: Chapman, 1966.

―――. *We Hold These Truths: Catholic Reflections on the American Proposition*. Kansas City, MO: Sheed and Ward, 1960.

Nagel, Thomas. *The Last Word: Philosophical Essays*. Oxford: Oxford University Press, 1997.

National Church Life Survey (Australia). Sydney: NCLS Research, 1996.

National Church Life Survey (Australia). Sydney: NCLS Research, 2001.

National Institute for Population and Social Security Research. *Population Projections for Japan 2001–2050*. 2003.

Newman, John Henry. *Apologia Pro Vita Sua* (1865). New York: Image Books, 1956.

―――. *Letter to the Duke of Norfolk* (1875). In *The Genius of John Henry Newman: Selections from His Writings*. Ed. Ian Ker. Oxford: Clarendon Press, 1989.

―――. *The Idea of a University* (1873). Ed. Ian Ker. Oxford: Clarendon Press, 1976.

―――. *The Idea of a University*. Ed. Martin J. Svaglic. South Bend, IN: University of Notre Dame Press, 1982.

Newsome, David. *The Convert Cardinals: John Henry Newman and Henry Edward Manning*. London: John Murray 1995.

Nietzsche, Friedrich. *Ecce Homo* (1908). In *The Anti-Christ, Ecce Homo, Twilight of the Idols and Other Writings*. Ed. Aaron Ridley and Judith Norman. Trans. Judith Norman. Cambridge: Cambridge University Press, 2005.

—————. *The Anti-Christ* (1889). In *The Anti-Christ, Ecce Homo, Twilight of the Idols and Other Writings*. Ed. Aaron Ridley and Judith Norman. Trans. Judith Norman. Cambridge: Cambridge University Press, 2005.

—————. *The Gay Science* (1882). Ed. Bernard Williams. Trans. Josefine Nauckhoff and Adrian Del Caro. Cambridge: Cambridge University Press, 2001.

—————. *Twilight of the Idols* (1889). In *The Anti-Christ, Ecce Homo, Twilight of the Idols and Other Writings*. Ed. Aaron Ridley and Judith Norman. Trans. Judith Norman. Cambridge: Cambridge University Press, 2005.

Norris, Pippa, and Ronald Inglehart. *Sacred and Secular: Religion and Politics Worldwide*. Cambridge: Cambridge University Press, 2005.

Novak, Michael. "Awakening from Nihilism: The Templeton Prize Address." *First Things* 45 (August–September 1994): 18–22.

—————. *On Cultivating Liberty: Reflections on Moral Ecology*. Lanham, MD: Rowman and Littlefield, 1999.

Oderberg, David, ed. *Form and Matter: Themes in Contemporary Metaphysics*. Malden, MA: Blackwells, 1999.

O'Hear, Anthony. *Beyond Evolution*. Oxford: Clarendon Press, 1997.

Oman, D., and D. Reed. "Religion and Mortality among the Community-Dwelling Elderly." *American Journal of Public Health* 88:10 (October 1998): 1469–75.

Parliament of the Commonwealth of Australia, House of Representatives Standing Committee on Legal and Constitutional Affairs. *To Have and To Hold: Strategies to Strengthen Marriage and Relationships*. Canberra: 1998.

Parry, Richard Lloyd. "Old World Order." *Australian Magazine, Weekend Australian*, 8–9 January 2000.

Peach, Hedley G. "Religion, Spirituality and Health: How Should Australia's Medical Professionals Respond?" *Medical Journal of Australia* 178:2 (20 January 2003): 86–88.

Pell, George. "*Rerum novarum* One Hundred Years Later." Boston University: Boston Conversazione, 1992.

Peterson, Peter G. *Gray Dawn*. New York: Times Books, 1999.

Plamenatz, John. *Man and Society: A Critical Examination of Political Thought from Machiavelli to Marx*. Vol. 3: *Hegel, Marx and the Idea of Progress*. New York: Longman, 1992.

Planned Parenthood of South Eastern Pennsylvania et al. *v. Casey, Governor of Pennsylvania*, et al. 505 US 833 (1992).

Pontifical Council for the Family. *On the Decrease of Fertility in the World*. 27 February 1998.

Ramsay, Hayden. "The Philosophical Significance of *Fides et ratio.*" *Philippiniana Sacra* 34:100 (January–April 1999): 79–91.

Ratzinger, Joseph. "Christianity: The Victory of Intelligence over the World of Religions." *30 Days* 1 (2000): 33–44.

Rawls, John. *A Theory of Justice.* Cambridge, MA: Belknap Press, 1971.

Ridley, Matt. *The Origins of Virtue: Human Instincts and the Evolution of Cooperation.* London: Penguin, 1998.

Rieff, Philip. *Fellow Teachers.* 3rd ed. Chicago: University of Chicago Press, 1985.

Roberts, L., I. Ahmed, and S. Hall "Intercessory Prayer for the Alleviation of Ill Health." *Cochrane Database of Systematic Reviews* 2000, Issue 2. Art. No.: CD000368.

Rorty, Richard. *Contingency, Irony, and Solidarity.* Cambridge: Cambridge University Press, 1989.

Rowland, Tracey. *Culture and the Thomist Tradition after Vatican II.* London: Routledge, 2003.

Rummel, Rudolph J. *Death by Government.* New Brunswick, NJ: Transaction, 1994.

Schall, James V., S.J. "The Culture of Modernity and Catholicism." *Homiletic and Pastoral Review* (June 2007): 8–19.

Schindler, David L. *Heart of the World, Center of the Church.* Edinburgh: T. and T. Clark, 1996.

Schmitt, Carl. *The Concept of the Political* (1932). Trans. George Schwab (1975). Chicago: University of Chicago Press, 1996.

Second Vatican Council. Declaration on Religious Freedom, *Dignitatis humanae.* 1965.

———. Pastoral Constitution on the Church in the Modern World, *Gaudium et spes.* 1965.

Sloan, R. P., E. Bagiella, and T. Powell. "Religion, Spirituality and Medicine." *Lancet* 353:9153 (20 February 1999): 664–67.

Sloan, R. P., et al. "Should Physicians Prescribe Religious Activities?" *New England Journal of Medicine* 342:25 (22 June 2000): 1913–16.

Smart J. J. C., and J. J. Haldane. *Atheism and Theism.* Oxford: Blackwells, 1996.

Solzhenitsyn, Aleksandr. *The Gulag Archipelago.* Abridged ed. Ed. Edward E. Ericson Jr. Trans. Thomas P. Whitney and Harry Willetts. London: Collins Harvill, 1986.

Souza, Raymond J. de. "Thinly Disguised Totalitarianism." *First Things* 142 (April 2004): 9–12.

Specter, Michael. "Population Implosion Worries a Graying Europe." *New York Times,* 10 July 1998.

Stannard, Russell. "God and the Big Bang." *Tablet,* 22–29 April 2000.

———. "Traces of a Designer." *Tablet,* 6 May 2000.

———. "Who'd Swap with the Sun?" *Tablet,* 13 May 2000.

Stark, Rodney. *For the Glory of God.* Princeton, NJ: Princeton University Press, 2003.

———. *The Victory of Reason.* New York: Random House, 2005.

Statistics New Zealand. *Demographic Trends 2004.* Wellington: Statistics New Zealand, 2004.

Stein, Harry. "Daytime Television Gets Judgmental." *City Journal,* Spring 2004. www.city-journal.org.

Steiner, George. *In Bluebeard's Castle.* London: Faber and Faber, 1971.

Strauss, Leo. *Natural Right and History* (1950). Chicago: University of Chicago Press, 1965.

Sulloway, Frank J. "Darwinian Virtues." *New York Review of Books,* 9 April 1998, 34–40.

Swope, Paul. "Abortion: A Failure to Communicate." *First Things* 82 (April 1998): 31–35.

"Thought Crime Becomes a Reality in Canada: An Interview with Michael O'Brien." www.ignatiusinsight.com.

Tocqueville, Alexis de. *Democracy in America* (1835 and 1840). Ed. and trans. Harvey C. Mansfield and Delba Winthrop. Chicago: University of Chicago Press, 2000.

Todorov, Tzvetan. "The Surrender to Nature." *New Republic,* 27 April 1998.

UNAIDS. *2006 Report on the Global AIDS Epidemic.* 2006.

United Nations, Department of Economic and Social Affairs, Population Division. *Replacement Migration: Is It a Solution to Declining and Aging Populations?* 2000.

———. *World Population in 2300.* 2004.

———. *World Population Prospects: The 1996 Revision.* 1997.

———. *World Population Prospects: The 2004 Revision.* 2005.

Vaus, David de. *Diversity and Change in Australian Families: Statistical Profiles.* Melbourne: Australian Institute of Family Studies, 2004.

Vaus, David de, Lixia Qu, and Ruth Weston. "Premarital Cohabitation and Subsequent Marital Stability." *Family Matters* 65 (Winter 2003): 34–39.

Weber, Max. "Politics as a Vocation" (1919). In *From Max Weber: Essays in Sociology.* Ed. and trans. H. H. Gerth and C. Wright Mills. London: Routledge and Kegan Paul, 1948.

Weigel, George. "The Free and Virtuous Society: Catholic Social Doctrine in the Twenty-First Century." The Fourth Annual Tyburn Lecture. Tyburn Convent, London, 19 May 2004.

———. *Witness to Hope: The Biography of Pope John Paul II.* New York: Harper Collins, 1999.

Wilson, Edward O. *Consilience: The Unity of Knowledge.* New York: Alfred A. Knopf, 1998.

———. *On Human Nature.* Cambridge, MA: Harvard University Press, 1978.

Zimmerman, Sacha. "Fetal Position." *New Republic,* 18 and 25 August 2003.

INDEX

Abelard, Peter, 146
abortion, x, 3, 16, 17, 19, 21, 29, 45, 46,
   50, 70, 71, 73, 74, 165; in Australia,
   112, 113; and the pro-life movement,
   109, 113, 115, 120, 124–25, 172–73;
   strategies about, 115–17
Acton, (John Emerich Edward
   Dalberg-Acton) first baron of,
   35–36, 37, 42
agnostic, 12, 88, 167
Alaric the Goth, ix
Anglicanism, 1, 54, 165; in Australia,
   110–12, 114, 143
Aquinas, Saint Thomas, 19, 44, 60, 96,
   132–33, 163
Aristotle, 89, 96
Arnold, Matthew, 14
assisted reproductive technology, 74,
   112
atheism, atheist, 11, 13, 15, 167
Augustine, Saint, ix; *City of God*, ix,
   xi, 43
Australian Labor Party, 1, 3, 55
authority, 17, 26, 43, 44, 61, 115, 120, 162

Barnes, Brian (archbishop of Port
   Moresby), 26
Beatitudes, the, 28
Behe, Michael, 95
Benedict XVI, 4
Beran, Josef Cardinal (archbishop of
   Prague), 2
Berlin, Isaiah, 45–46
Bible, the. *See* God; John, Saint;
   Mark, Saint; Matthew, Saint; New
   Testament; Old Testament; Paul,
   Saint

bioethics, 60, 63
Burke, Edmund, 36
business. *See* economics, the economy

Calvinism, 71
Catholic Church, the. *See* Catholicism
Catholic schools, 1, 55, 114, 124
Catholic social teaching, 26, 28–29,
   147, 166–67
Catholicism, x, 29, 30, 45, 60, 67, 149,
   155, 159, 161, 163, 165, 168, 173–74; in
   Australia, 1–2, 66, 110–12, 113–14,
   141–43, 166; and democracy, x,
   56–57, 60, 63, 64–65, 168; and
   science, 90; teachings of, x, 63–64,
   92, 121–22, 142, 154, 158–59. *See also*
   rights
celibacy, 123–24
Chekov, Anton, 40
Chesnais, Jean-Claude, 79, 107
Chesterton, G. K. (Gilbert Keith),
   57n10
Christianity, 30, 44, 59, 67, 80, 89,
   90–91, 92, 98, 101, 124, 148, 159,
   165; in Australia, 42; evangelical,
   2, 54, 111, 114; not an ideology, 76;
   and myth, 146–47; realism of, 71,
   81; witness of, 51, 63, 125, 137. *See also*
   philosophy; religion
Churchill, Sir Winston, 64
cloning, 112
common good, the, 16, 19, 24, 33, 46,
   53, 59, 62, 65, 79, 81, 83, 167, 173
Communism, 14, 38, 39–40, 42, 46, 55,
   63, 82, 97. *See also* totalitarianism
contraception, 46, 67, 69, 71, 121, 158,
   165

New Testament, 45, 160, 167, 170.
  See also John, Saint; Mark, Saint;
  Matthew, Saint; Paul, Saint
Newman, Blessed John Henry
  (Cardinal), 36, 146–56; *Apologia Pro
  Vita Sua*, 155; on conscience, 164; *The
  Idea of a University*, 146; *Letter to the
  Duke of Norfolk*, 160, 163–64
Nietzsche, Friedrich, 14, 68, 152, 170,
  173
nihilism, 23, 89, 172
Novak, Michael, 20, 23
Nussbaum, Martha, 10n1

O'Hear, Anthony, 92, 132
Old Testament, 13
Origen, 88
Orwell, George, 50; *1984*, 50
Ozanam, Blessed Frédéric, 7n10

pagan, paganism, 15, 148–49
Pascal, Blaise, 130
passion, 33
Paul, Saint, 45, 160
Paul VI, 121, 159; *Humanae vitae*, 158, 159
peace, 38, 49, 51, 78
philosophy, 30, 56, 89, 90, 124, 132, 133,
  144; and Christianity, 132–35, 147;
  and theology, 152–53
Pilate, Pontius, 170
Pius IX, 36; *Syllabus errorum* 36
Pius X, Saint, 1; *Vehementer nos*, 1
Pius XII, 2,
Pol Pot (Saloth Sar), 15, 41
politics, xi, 25, 33, 37, 63, 73, 83;
  responsibility of lay people for, 4,
  26, 65; role of church leaders and
  clergy in, 28–29, 31–32, 55, 65
population. *See* demographic decline
pornography, 21, 22, 73, 74
postmodernism, postmodernist, 89,
  118

Powell, Frederick, 35
power, 16, 25, 26, 35, 36, 72, 78, 79,
  170, 173
prostitution, 21
psychoanalysis. *See* Freud, Sigmund

rationalism, 14, 126
Rawls, John, 10n1, 72, 162
Reagan, Ronald, 52, 111
reason, 4 , 47, 81, 119, 153, 172; and
  evolution, 92–93; and religion 10–11,
  118, 147, 149, 150, 166–67. *See also*
  faith; God
relativism, 9, 18–19, 23, 47–48, 57, 77,
  118, 119, 120, 169, 170
religion, 15, 25, 40, 47, 78, 90, 97, 148,
  149, 161; in Australia, 52, 109–12;
  freedom of, 162; key moral tasks
  of, 30; and knowledge, 150, 151, 152,
  153; political substitutes for, 83;
  privatization of, 3, 54–56, 167; and
  science, 89, 96–97, 98, 100–101, 126,
  144. *See also* democracy; freedom;
  reason
religious belief, xi, 27, 90, 109, 111–12,
  113; advantages of, 137–44
revelation, 11, 44, 150, 153, 156, 167
Ridley, Matt, 91–92
Rieff, Philip, 71
rights, 4, 5, 32, 45, 47, 54, 58, 61-63,
  71, 78, 90, 124, 157–58, 161, 167–74;
  children's, 62; claims to primacy
  of, 169; confusion about, 18–19;
  foundations of, 18, 37, 169, 171;
  to life, 16, 19, 62, 169, 172; moral
  appeal of, 17, 62; and moral
  realism, 65; secular and Catholic
  understandings of, 59–60, 61,
  167–68, 173. *See also* freedom; human
  person; law
Rousseau, Jean-Jacques, 76
Rorty, Richard, 73, 152, 171–72

Voltaire (François-Marie Arouet),
88, 90

Watson, James, 95
Weber, Max, 12, 33
Weigel, George, 73, 120
Whewell, William, 87
Wickramasinghe, Chandra, 130
Wilberforce, Samuel (bishop of
Oxford), 13, 88

Wilson, Edward, 87, 88, 89, 91, 94,
96–97, 98–99, 100–101; *Consilience*,
87, 98; and sociobiology, 90
Wojtyła, Karol, 121. *See also* John
Paul II
Woodstock, 49–50, 51
Wyszilski, Stefan Cardinal
(archbishop of Warsaw), 2

God & Caesar: Selected Essays on Religion, Politics, & Society was designed and typeset in Centaur with Charlemagne display type by Kachergis Book Design of Pittsboro, North Carolina. It was printed on 60-pound Natures Natural and bound by Thomson-Shore of Dexter, Michigan.